REFLUX 101

Reflux 101

A PARENTS GUIDE TO GASTROESOPHAGEAL REFLUX

JAN GAMBINO, M.ED.

Published in the United States by lulu.com
www.refluxmom.com

Cover Design: Reed Graphics, Inc./www.reedgraphics.com
Cover photo: istockphoto.com/Leigh Schlindler
Author Photo: Pam Creaturo

Send inquires to:
The Reflux Mom
P.O. Box 171
Arnold, Maryland 21012
www.refluxmom.com.

Library of Congress Cataloging-Publication Data
Reflux 101: A Parents guide to gastroesophageal reflux / Jan Gambino—1st ed.
1. Reflux . 2. Gastroesophageal reflux. 3. Medicine—Pediatric . I. Gambino, Jan
Library of Congress Control Number 2008937623
ISBN: 978-0-557-02870-2
PRINTED IN THE UNITED STATES OF AMERICA
First Edition

Disclaimer: This book is not a substitute for medical care and advice. Please consult your
physician before starting, modifying or discontinuing any medication or treatment.

THIS BOOK IS DEDICATED TO

EMILY, JENNA AND REBECCA

►With Special Thanks…

I am grateful to everyone who offered support and guidance while I wrote this book. First, I would like to thank my parents, Patricia and Richard Gambino, and siblings Jeffrey Gambino, Pamela Creaturo, Donna Gambino and their families for their love, support and guidance. A special thank you to my beautiful daughters Emily, Jenna and Rebecca for enduring the ups and downs of book writing and allowing me to share the secrets of their digestive systems in an effort to help others.

Thank you to my editor Michelle LeFurge for assisting me with every aspect of the book writing process and helping me transform hundreds of stories and conversations with parents into a handbook. Her support and patience went way above and beyond the duties of book editor!

I would like to thank Paulette Forbes for copyediting and Marie Bialousz of Reed Graphics, Inc. for the wonderful cover and logo designs.

My boundless thanks to the professionals who provided important feedback on the book: Joan Comrie, M.S. CCC-SLP, Suzanne Evans Morris, Ph.D., John Latimer, MD and Polly Tarbell, Med CCC-SLP.

The wonderful staff of The HealthCentral Network gave me the opportunity to share my stories about reflux on the *www.healthcentral.com* website and in this book. Thank you for your enthusiasm and support.

And, to my colleagues, the hundreds of parents, grandparents and friends of babies and children with reflux from around the world, thank you for sharing your concerns, questions and stories with me. A special thank you is extended to Mary Biden Bourgeois, Stephanie Doersam, Pam Tyler, Amy Arnold, Stephanie Petters, Annette Pic and Jessica Penkert for sharing their personal stories. You have taught me so much about caring for a child with reflux.

▶ TABLE OF CONTENTS

► ENTERING AND USING THIS BOOK

This is the book I wish I had when struggling with my daughter's reflux. Like every parent, I wished my girls came with a set of instructions. This is especially true when you have a baby or child with gastroesophageal reflux. By using the "voice of experience" — my own and hundreds of other parents coping with their children who have GER and GERD — my focus has been to make you feel less isolated and better ready to take on your unplanned career as caretaker. I hope this book will be your source for information and support on all aspects of caring for a baby or child with reflux from birth to age 12 years, guiding you through a difficult season of parenting.

Before you begin reading, please remember that the information in this book is not a substitute for medical advice. It is important to always consult a physician or other medical professional for an accurate diagnosis and appropriate treatment plan. Do not try any treatment, positioning or medication described in this book without first discussing the information with your doctor. You and your doctor (or doctors) are a team. Each part of this book has specific chapters or parts of chapters on how best to work with your medical team. Every parent of a child with reflux has felt the frustration, isolation and, yes, anger and fear when working through the diagnosis and treatment of your sick baby. You are not alone. You are a critical member of "Team Reflux."

As you choose where in this book to begin, perhaps you will begin with the table of contents; it is designed for you to go directly to your information needs, as is the index. Another alternative is to start with what you need to know and read the part of the book that relates best to your child. As a ready way to accomplish this, I have organized this book to allow you to enter gently, beginning with GER. Gastroesophageal Reflux or GER is a normal physiologic event in infancy and often causes spit up and occasional vomiting episodes. The vast majority of babies with spit up have GER, requiring extra care and added stress but not medical treatment. Part 1 provides a full description of terminology and definitions used to describe GER. If your baby has GER, Parts 2 through 4 may only be for future reference. I certainly hope so!

If you are adding Part 2 to your reading, you will be there because your doctor has diagnosed GERD. Gastroesophageal Reflux Disease or GERD is reflux that has caused complications such as esophageal damage. There is a huge difference between GER and GERD diagnosis, treatments and outcomes. In Part 2 you will find specific information on the diagnosis and treatment of GERD. It will also guide you through parent-tested home care and survival tips to deal with this condition and its impact on you and your family.

In Part 3 you will find a discussion of older children and children with complex medical issues related to gastroesophageal reflux disease. For specific information on tests, medications and surgery, turn to Part 4. If you have a baby with GER, you will save yourself a lot of worry by skipping Part 4; most of what it offers won't apply to your child. Treat it more as a "go to" place on a need to know basis.

Lastly, a resource list provides information on books, products and organizations of interest to parents. I use the pronoun "she" throughout the book, perhaps because my refluxers were girls! Also, for the most part, I will use the term "reflux" in the book because it sounds less clinical and is the word that most parents use in every day conversation. I will occasionally use the term reflux event or reflux episode where appropriate to describe isolated incidences of backwashing.

I hope this book will offer you comfort and hope as you care for your baby or child with reflux. I wrote this book for parents because I longed for a book to guide me when my daughter was struggling with reflux and the typical parenting books were of little use to me.

Jan Gambino

PART 1 ▶ GER

1 ▶ SYMPTOMS AND DIAGNOSIS OF GER

It is likely that many of you sat in high school science class and thought, "I will never need to know any of this information!" Fast forward to parenthood, and perhaps now you are wishing you could remember more about the lecture on digestion. For those of you who are too tired to remember your phone number, much less what you learned in high school, this chapter will give you a refresher course. So welcome to anatomy class...again.

Remember, if this chapter still leaves you with questions about the mechanics of reflux, ask your doctor for a quick refresher class. All of those colorful charts and pictures in exam rooms are not just for decoration. She went to medical school so she is most qualified to relay this information and explain the fancy terminology.

What is Normal Digestion?

To explain gastroesophageal reflux, we will begin with a lesson on the normal functioning of the digestive system. Eating is often referred to as natural and instinctive, but it actually requires a very intricate series of coordinated movements.

We begin our digestive process with the desire for food: the brain signals that it is time to eat and our nose smells food, stimulating our appetite. Our saliva glands wet the food, making it easier for our teeth to chew. The tongue and jaw manipulate the food as we chew and move the food to the back of the throat. When food reaches the back of the tongue, a sensory trigger causes a reflexive swallow. At the same time, the soft palate elevates to keep food out of the nose and the epiglottis lowers to cover the airway. A muscle at the top of the esophagus (food pipe) opens to let food enter and move toward the stomach.

After the food is swallowed, the rest of digestion takes place automatically and is not under conscious control. The esophagus produces mucus to help the food slide down better and the esophageal muscles contract with a wave-like motion to squeeze the food downward toward the stomach. This action, called "peristalsis" is what makes it possible to swallow even if you are up side down. Just above the stomach is a particularly well developed ring of muscles, the Lower Esophageal Sphincter or LES. The LES must relax to allow food to pass from the esophagus to the stomach and then tighten and remain tight until more food arrives from the mouth. The LES may also open to allow the release of air from the stomach in the form of a burp or belch.

When food and drink reach the stomach, special cells in the lining of the stomach secrete acid and digestive enzymes. The stomach is not digested by these caustic chemicals because it is protected by a layer of mucus. The stomach stretches slowly to accommodate the food (gastric accommodation) and then signals the body to stop eating when it is full.

The stomach muscles start squeezing, grinding and churning the food to break it into smaller parts. Soft foods and liquids trigger milder squeezing and solid foods trigger vigorous churning action. Liquids are absorbed by the walls of the stomach and solid food is then ground into small particles by the stomach. When the stomach is finished grinding the food to little pieces, a similar ring of muscles at the bottom of the stomach allows the food to move into the small intestine at a controlled rate. This ring is called the pylorus.

The time it takes to digest food varies greatly from person to person and from meal to meal. Fatty foods and tough foods like meat and seeds stay in the stomach longer than mushy foods or liquids.

When the food is in the small intestine, it mixes with enzymes, bile and alkaline secretions which help to break up the food and release the nutrients. The pancreas and the liver make enzymes and bile that are stored in the gall bladder. Most of the nutrients are absorbed through the wall of the small intestine and the waste passes into the large intestine where the water is removed so the waste gets more solid.

What is Gastroesophageal Reflux (GER)?

Gastroesophageal Reflux or GER is defined as the backwashing of stomach contents into the esophagus and throat during or after a meal. Quite literally, it is

Gastro (stomach) + Esophageal (food tube) + Reflux (backwash)

This expelling of the stomach contents is a normal event for an infant, especially after over eating. This backwash can take the form of a wet burp, spit up or vomiting that empties the stomach and does not cause pain or distress to the baby. GER (sometimes referred to as "physiologic reflux") is not a disease - it is a normal process that can happen to everybody — babies, as well as older children and adults. A toddler or an older child may burp or belch after a meal or have the sensation of food coming up. Again, this is a normal event, and it may occur after over eating or engaging in physical activity after a meal.

We know that most babies spit up on a regular basis. But when a baby has frequent spit up episodes, parents get quite worried. Rest assured that *occasional* reflux episodes are very seldom cause for alarm. Even a bit of spitting up after every meal can be perfectly harmless (at least to the baby). Doctors often refer to otherwise healthy babies who spit up as "happy spitters." GER in infancy is common. With conservative measures, such as positioning and home care, it usually gets better by six months of age.

INFANT ANATOMY AND GER

There are some common reasons why babies often have more reflux episodes then children and adults:

A baby has poor trunk control and underdeveloped abdominal muscles in the first months of life, leading to more reflux episodes.

A baby's stomach lacks the stretch/flexibility of an adult stomach. When a baby eats, the stomach cannot expand as well to accept the food

Babies tend to eat a large amount for their stomach size and a liquid meal

Babies spend a lot of time lying down, often when their stomachs are full.

Babies have a short esophagus compared to an adult.

WHAT CAUSES GER?

Causes of gastroesophageal reflux include:

Lower Esophageal Sphincter (LES) Relaxation: Under normal conditions, the LES relaxes to let out a burp or let in a swallow of food. During a reflux episode, the LES will relax too much and allow food and acid to escape from the stomach into the esophagus.

Poor Motility: The muscles and nerves in the esophagus need to tighten and relax in a coordinated fashion to allow food to pass through the esophagus and digest properly. Poor motility occurs when there is a lack of coordination in the nerves and muscles.

Immature Neurological System: Neurological impairment or prematurity can cause the brain to signal the LES to relax and contract at the wrong time.

Over-Eating: When your baby eats a very large meal, it can put pressure on the stomach and cause the food to push open the LES.

Hiatal Hernia: A hiatal hernia occurs when part of the stomach protrudes through the diaphragm and into the chest cavity. Food in the top stomach pouch gets squeezed between the lungs with every breath causing heartburn and pain.

Delayed Gastric Emptying: Gastroparesis (delayed gastric emptying) occurs when the nerves in the stomach are not

working properly and food stays in the stomach too long causing fullness and discomfort.

Intolerances and Allergies: Food allergies can cause the stomach to reject food, causing vomiting and irritation to the esophagus and stomach.

Constipation: Constipation can slow digestion and prevent food from leaving the stomach at a normal rate. It is just like the plumbing...if there is a clog somewhere, the whole system backs up.

WILL MY BABY OUTGROW REFLUX?

It is highly likely your baby will outgrow GER; approximately 80-90% of babies outgrow reflux in the first year of life. Many infants show improvement around four to six months of age when their digestive systems mature and they are able to sit up independently and control their muscles. Other babies are on the one year or even the two year plan before their digestive system can manage food gracefully.

IS IT GENETIC?

There is evidence that some families have a genetic form of GERD with a pattern of multiple generations (siblings, aunts, uncles, grandparents, etc) affected. Since most babies have GER or physiologic reflux in infancy, only a smaller group of families are affected by the genetic form of GERD (gastroesophageal reflux disease).

WILL IT HAPPEN AGAIN?

After having one baby with reflux, many weary parents are sure they would never have the stamina to risk bringing another baby with reflux into their family. Since GER or

---

GERD Parents Say:

It is really hard the second time around, I will be honest. But there is a difference in that you do know it will end someday and that kind of gets you through the day.

◆

Make your GI appointments when you are 8 months pregnant!

◆

I knew what was happening and marched right in to the doctor to begin treatment.

◆

I personally think in many ways it is easier the next time around. You are more knowledgeable and know how to help your hurting baby. It's the parents who have a perfect baby first who are in for a wild ride when their second is a refluxer.

---

physiologic reflux is very common in infancy, it is possible to have more than one child with reflux.

Most parents find that the first child with reflux provided all the necessary training and it is somehow seems easier the next time. Perhaps you will begin home care earlier. It is likely you and the doctor will be familiar with each other (from baby #1), so getting an appointment and communicating your concerns will be far easier.

WHAT IS GASTROESOPHAGEAL REFLUX DISEASE (GERD)?

The North American Society for Pediatric Gastroenterology, Hepatology and Nutrition (NASPGHAN) defines Gastroesophageal Reflux Disease as "...symptoms or complications of Gastroesophageal Reflux. Clinical manifestations of GERD in children include vomiting, poor weight gain, dysphagia, abdominal or substernal pain, esophagitis and respiratory disorders."

Your doctor will evaluate your baby or child to determine if the symptoms suggest GER or GERD. Thankfully, most babies who show symptoms have GER, a normal condition that often resolves spontaneously in the first few months of life without medical intervention. A much smaller percentage of babies have GERD with symptoms that persist into childhood. Recent data suggests that several million children in the United States have GERD.

Too often we think of *adult* gastroesophageal reflux as the same experience as infant gastroesophageal reflux. Not true. In adults, acid overproduction and esophageal injury are far more common and are considered indicators of GERD.

Babies and children with GER are monitored for signs of complications and esophageal injury associated with a diagnosis of GERD.

GERD Myth: A faulty valve causes reflux

Some people believe the place where the esophagus meets the stomach has a flap that closes to prevent food from coming up. The area where the esophagus meets the stomach is called the Lower Esophageal Sphincter (LES). It is a ring of muscles instead of a flap. When food enters the stomach, the muscles tighten so the food cannot escape. Reflux occurs when the LES fails to tighten or opens slightly, allowing food to enter into the esophagus.

2 ▶ SYMPTOMS AND DIAGNOSIS OF GER

Your gut tells you something is wrong. Your baby doesn't act like her big sister or the baby next door. You wonder if you're right to worry...and worry that you might be right! So, you go with your gut. By reading this book, you are taking the first step to diagnosis and treatment. Here we will explore what might be GER symptoms. Don't be frustrated if others tell you "all babies have that." Let a diagnosis of "happy spitter" be your pleasant reward for being cautious.

Is it GER... or GERD?

After reading chapter 1 you may still be confused about the differences between GER and GERD. The reality is, GER and GERD may look the same in the first few days or weeks. Most doctors consider a diagnosis of GER since it is more common and therefore the most likely cause of the symptoms. You can see why it is so difficult for parents and doctors to diagnose and treat reflux. It may take days or weeks of observation to see a pattern of symptoms. GER and GERD can have mild to severe symptoms. Some babies have a few classic symptoms while others have more subtle or atypical symptoms. Sorting out GER from GERD is a process you and your doctor will work on together. If it is GERD, the second half of this book will be very important.

> ### A GER Mom asks:
>
> The other mom in the waiting room said her son spits up after each meal but my baby hardly ever needs a burp cloth after a feeding. How can they both have reflux?

Only your doctor can diagnose GER or GERD. The description of symptoms is meant to guide you in your discussion of symptoms with your doctor.

It can be frustrating when the symptoms change a bit from day to day. Sometimes these changes can be important clues that will help you identify something like a food that causes symptoms. Other times, the reflux may just flare up or subside for no reason at all.

As reflux starts to go away, the symptoms may be more uneven from day to day. It can be very stressful when a flare

Infant GER	GERD
Normal condition common in infancy	A common *childhood disease*
Resolves during infancy	A *chronic* condition.
Symptoms include regurgitation and vomiting	*Symptoms* cause complications
Testing not needed	*Testing* may or may not be needed.
Treatment is supportive and may include homecare	*Treatment* may include homecare, diet, medication and surgery (rare).

up happens after a quiet week or two and you were starting to think the reflux was gone. It probably is going away – just not in nice, neat steps.

Noticing Symptoms in Infants and Toddlers

Even though your baby has left the womb, it is likely that you and the baby are pretty much attached to each other, as if the cord had not been cut. Nobody else spends as much time with your baby and nobody else can see her symptoms as well as you can. It is likely that you had a hunch something was not right well before everyone else. Doctors know parents can be the best observers of their child's symptoms. Parents often notice things about their child that nobody else could.

A GER Mom says:

Within a few days of my daughter's birth, I knew something wasn't quite right. Often, I would cry and tell my husband there was something wrong with our baby. Everyone assumed I just had postpartum depression. But I listened to my gut and searched all over the bookstore and internet until I figured out what was troubling my baby. It wasn't easy because she didn't have the classic signs of reflux.

This makes you a very important part of your baby's medical team. The doctor only spends a few minutes with your baby during check ups so it is important to report all symptoms and observations about behavior at home. All of those little observations are clues for the doctor and may make a huge difference in determining treatment. The doctor depends on you to provide this information.

These three categories of symptoms are what will send you into your baby's doctor for answers.

SPIT UP AND VOMITING

Parents and physicians spend a great deal of time discussing spit up and vomiting. The common definition of *spit up* is a small amount of stomach contents dripping or spitting out of the mouth after a meal. Most babies with reflux tend to spit up quite a bit. A doctor may refer to spit up as regurgitation.

Vomiting is the more forceful release of stomach contents and is often associated with expelling most or all of the meal. It is important to let your baby's doctor know if she is vomiting. While *spit up* is normal and expected in infancy, vomiting is not.

In some cases, a baby or toddler may have *projectile vomiting*. This is a more forceful, often violent form of vomiting. Babies have been known to vomit clear across the room (right onto the new sofa of course) and may even vomit forcefully out of the nose and mouth at the same time. Occasional episodes of projectile vomiting are not uncommon, but it is always frightening to parents. Be sure to report projectile vomiting episodes to your doctor, as it is sometimes a sign of a more serious problem such as pyloric stenosis.

Burps, Hiccups and Other Loud Noises

A Reflux Dad says:

When my son refluxes, it sounds like hiccups. If he starts to have a distressed look on his face and his little arms start waving, I know it is time to get ready for the whole meal to come up.

Your baby may not spit up at all. She might just have wet burps, wet hiccups or you might hear food coming part way up her throat. Some parents report that they can hear loud rumbling and strange noises coming from the very tiny digestive systems of their babies. The burps and hiccups may be quite painful for some babies. Parents quickly learn what all of these gurgles and burps mean.

CRYING

Lets face it, all babies cry. Some babies seem to cry more than others especially in the first few months of life. Parents and doctors spend a great deal of time discussing crying and whether the crying signals a problem or not. Babies cry when they are tired, wet and hungry. Some babies are highly sensitive to their environment and may cry when they are overwhelmed by noise and light or movement. Babies also cry to signal distress such as pain, discomfort and illness. It is clear that GERD may be very painful to babies and cause prolonged bouts of crying and fussing. However, it isn't clear why some babies with GER seem to cry and fuss as well. There is some concern in the medical community that all infant crying is being attributed to GERD and that babies are being overly medicated. It isn't clear why some babies experience distress during episodes of spit up or vomiting and other babies are called "happy spitters."

Babies cry to communicate their needs. We often wish they could be more specific in their communication! Since babies cannot tell us exactly what is wrong, parents and doctors are left guessing the source of discomfort. A baby may have one or many pain issues such as ear infections, colic or constipation along with reflux.

Some babies are "high need" and seem to be more easily distressed by noise and other environmental factors. Be sure you and the doctor have addressed other reasons for crying and distress before focusing just on reflux as the cause for all pain. In addition, there are books on calming and comforting a fussy baby. Some parents have had a great deal of success with these techniques.

Looks Like ... Could be...

In this world of medical miracles, we expect that there must be a test for every ailment. If the test is positive, you have a clear diagnosis and treatment begins.

Yet the vast majority of infants and children are diagnosed with GER based on a visit to the doctor for a physical exam, a review of symptoms and a trial of home treatment. Some doctors worry that even babies with GER (or physiologic reflux) are being offered unnecessary medical treatment more commonly used to treat GERD. It is hoped that

> ### GER Moms Say:
>
> I called the pediatrician because I was worried about how much my baby was spitting up and how she would cry for an hour afterward. He told me that he could probably diagnose reflux on the phone that night, but he had me bring her in just to make sure it wasn't a virus.
>
> ◆
>
> I had never spent much time around other babies. I asked the doctor if her pattern of feeding and vomiting were normal.

19

research will lead to better methods of identifying babies who need medication and home care treatment, and those who would best benefit from home care treatment alone.

If your baby spits up excessively and cries a lot, you may have heard about reflux very early on. A nurse at the hospital or a neighbor may have been the first one to notice the classic signs of reflux.

Perhaps your pediatrician was the first to suggest reflux when you reported common symptoms such as excessive spitting up and excessive crying.

On the other hand, you may have noticed that your baby had symptoms of reflux, but you may not have known that they were signs of a problem. Unless you were familiar with the concept that babies can have reflux, you would have no reason be suspicious.

When you are talking to the doctor about reflux symptoms, keep in mind that there are many reasons for a baby to cry, spit up or vomit. Gastroesophageal reflux is just one of them. Your doctor will use his/her diagnostic tools and experience to determine the cause of the symptoms. Along with reflux, your baby's doctor will consider other conditions that have a pattern of symptoms similar to GER and GERD when making a diagnosis. Here are the most common.

> ### *Jan says:*
>
> I often ask pediatricians, "Do you have many patients with gastroesophageal reflux?" The typical responses are: "All of them!"... or ..."Doesn't *everyone* have reflux?!" ... or ... exaggerated eye rolling and a pained facial expression!

Colic: Colic is defined as excessive crying in infancy with no known cause. Colic tends to start a few weeks after birth and resolves spontaneously in the first few months of life. Colic may be related to infant temperament or an immature neurological/digestive system.

When diagnosing colic, doctors use the rule of threes: three hours of crying, three or more days per week, it starts at about three weeks and it usually stops fairly suddenly about three months after it started.

Unfortunately, colic and reflux may occur together. A researcher studying colic in babies found that 50% of the babies identified as having "colic" also had symptoms of reflux. Parents and doctors will have the added challenge of identifying and treating these symptoms.

Milk Soy Protein Intolerance: Milk Soy Protein Intolerance is caused by the inability of an infant to digest the protein in cow's milk and soy products leading to vomiting and blood in the stool.

Eosinophilic Esophagitis: Eosinophilic Esophagitis is caused by irritation to the esophagus from food allergies causing changes to the lining of the esophagus and symptoms that are suggestive of GERD.

Pyloric Stenosis: when the muscles in the lower part of the stomach (pyloris) become enlarged, preventing food from exiting the stomach and passing into the intestines.

Malrotation: A malrotation of the stomach is a rare birth defect in which the stomach appears to be upside down.

Don't get discouraged if it takes a few calls to the doctor and multiple office visits to sort out the symptoms. The doctor may need to see the pattern of symptoms over time to make a diagnosis.

3 ▶ GOING TO THE DOCTOR

If your baby is growing and looks and acts well, the doctor might suspect GER instead of GERD and recommend observing your baby. If your baby manages the symptoms without intervention, she probably has GER and no further treatment is needed. It is likely your doctor will ask you to bring the baby in more frequently to monitor the reflux symptoms. Your doctor is also counting on you to report any changes.

If your doctor wants to wait before starting treatment and you disagree, be sure to continue discussing the situation with her. Perhaps you could keep a journal and write down symptoms and patterns that you are seeing at home. Some babies act and look normal at the doctor's office and then scream and cry all night.

It is likely your pediatrician or family doctor is going to diagnose and treat reflux. Most babies and toddlers have typical reflux that responds easily to the standard home care

---

Jan says:

Sometimes parents tell me that the doctor doesn't seem concerned about a parent's report of symptoms during a well check up. Perhaps the concerns get lost when there are so many other topics to cover during a well check up such as shots and car seat safety. I often tell parents to schedule a separate "sick visit" just to address the concerns of pain, feeding and digestion.

---

treatments. It is important to schedule an appointment for a discussion of symptoms, an exam and weight check. You and the doctor can then develop a treatment plan.

Finding the Right Doctor

Before you had children, you probably spent little time in a doctor's office. Your first experience with ongoing medical care was having regular visits with the prenatal doctor followed by selecting a pediatrician. Now that your baby has some health issues, you may feel that you are constantly going to the doctor.

Jan says:

I was pretty angry and disillusioned at the medical system by the time I found an on line support group. After I met some other parents who really understood what I was going through, I began to realize that I was expecting too much of the doctors. They were providing excellent care for my daughter. I stopped looking to the doctors for emotional support because I had a circle of reflux moms to listen and support me.

You may be finding out about the complexities of the medical system including preauthorization for tests and treatment as well as co pays and eligibility rules. Some insurance companies require that a primary doctor, such as a pediatrician, serve as the gate keeper for medical care.

You and your child are going to be spending more time with the doctor than the typical pediatric patient. There may be extra phone consultations, office visits and weight checks. It is important to feel comfortable with the primary care physician and the office staff. The primary care office should have a telephone advice/call back system that is reliable so that you can relay information to the medical staff and receive a call back promptly (usually during the same day). You may want to talk with your doctor about the best time to call and how to handle an emergency after office hours.

The office staff and nurses should be respectful and courteous to you, even if you are a frequent customer. Caring for a child with reflux can change from day to day, and it is common to have frequent questions and concerns. It helps the office staff and doctor if a family member is the designated contact person. Do not hesitate to call during regular office hours for any problem, large or small.

Remember, it is the PRIMARY job of the doctor to provide medical care for your child. If you are lucky, your child's doctor may take on a support role to you and your family.

GER parents share about doctors

The biggest lesson I learned in all this is to find a physician who trusts your intuition as a mother and will listen to it. I know it can be hard for doctors to always put all the pieces together, but we know our kids best and we need them to listen when things aren't right.

◆

I feel like I have an excellent doctor because he listens, asks questions and then we make a team decision on treatment. I feel very involved and even if the answer I got was different from the one I predicted, I still feel very informed and involved.

◆

My favorite doctors are the ones that give you their time, so you don't feel rushed or get the impression that they have other, more important things to be doing. I have also been impressed when they call to check up on the kids after an illness or injury. Another big one is feeling like they truly care about you and your family.

If you find that the doctor is not providing the type of reassurance and support that you need as a parent, contacting a patient support organization can make a huge impact.

ADVOCATING FOR YOUR BABY

Some parents have a very strong instinct that something is "wrong" but they may not be able to figure out how to get someone to listen to them. It might be necessary to report the problem to the doctor several times before she understands that your baby needs treatment.

Practical Tips for Doctor Visits

Create a notebook or binder with all your notes and medical papers. Planning ahead and organizing your notes and records will go a long way toward ensuring a productive visit to the doctor.

Here's Jan's step-by-step approach to prepare for the doctor appointment:

Make a list of symptoms you see at home. Place a star next to the 3 most worrisome symptoms. These are the symptoms you really want to address with the doctor.

Bring a journal with a 3 day record of food intake, sleep patterns, fussy periods, crying, etc.

Bring your list of questions and do not leave until you have received an answer to each one.

Write down the doctor's answers and other recommendations.

IT'S ALL ABOUT COMMUNICATION

I often tell parents this story to illustrate the need to communicate clearly to the doctor. This is a story about two babies with the same symptoms. Each parent brings the baby to the doctor. However, each parent communicates with the doctor in a very different way. See what happens.

Parent A says, "My baby cries and spits up all the time." The doctor thinks, "I hear this from every parent of a new baby." The doctor tells the mother, "Watch him, and let me know if it gets worse. It is common for babies to cry and spit up in the newborn period."

Parent B opens her notebook and reads: "During the last three days, my baby cried 12-16 hours a day, vomited 1-2 ounces at each feeding and she wants to nurse 10-12 times a

26

day." The doctor thinks, *"I need to ask this parent more questions and find out why this baby is in such terrible pain."*

Which baby gets better care? It is likely that the first parent will go home thinking, "my doctor isn't very good" or "he/she doesn't get it" after being reassured that all babies cry. It is likely that Baby B will get a thorough exam following an in-depth discussion between the parent and the doctor. In addition, the second parent is likely to go home with a treatment plan and instructions for follow up. This parent will feel like the doctor is a partner in care.

DOCUMENTATION AND MEMORY TRIGGERS

Doctors like hard data. At each appointment, your doctor will most likely ask you specific questions such as, "How many ounces of formula were consumed each day?", or "How many times did she vomit?" If you are already exhausted from limited sleep and too much to do, it may be difficult to remember what happened an hour ago, much less last week.

Jan says:

About once a month, I would write down all of the foods my toddler ate in a day. I could compare her eating from a month or even 6 months ago and see such big changes. Perhaps she had increased the amount of food she ate at one meal or started eating food from another food group. In the day to day struggles, it was hard to see that we were making progress in her eating and that she was eating and drinking more over time.

Many parents find it helpful to keep a diary or notebook where they write down information. Use a system that allows you to write quickly. For instance, if you have to give a medication three times a day, write down the name of the medication and place a check next to it after you have given each dose. This will help you remember the schedule as well as give you a record to bring to the doctor.

A calendar on the refrigerator can also be used to write important information. You can create a simple checklist to record information, such as: number of feedings and amount per day, amount of crying and sleep, vomiting, burping, and medications or other treatments given.

TAKE A SNAPSHOT

Once in a while, pick a typical day for your child and record typical feeding, foods eaten, naps, sleep and reflux symptoms. Some parents literally bring in a picture to illustrate

---

... Try this ...

In addition to listing all my daughter's symptoms in writing, I brought a video of my daughter during an episode of projectile vomiting. He was surprised at the forcefulness of her vomiting and ordered a test to rule out Pyloric Stenosis.

---

the extent of the problem. When you are busy taking care of so much during the day, it may be difficult to observe patterns and see progress.

BRING A LIST OF QUESTIONS

Bring a list of questions to each appointment so you will not forget to ask something important. Tell the doctor you have a list of questions and make sure you have the opportunity to

---

A GER Mom says:

I always bring a pad of paper and pen to write down information we discuss at the appointment. I also repeat certain things that he says: "So, you are saying..." to make sure that I understand what he is recommending.

---

go through your entire list. If the doctor is getting ready to end the appointment, you can remind him/her that you have a few more questions.

When you leave the appointment, you should know the following:

Diagnosis
Treatment
Plan for follow up

How to reach the doctor with questions/concerns

Bring Another Adult with You

Whether this is your weekly pediatrician appointment or you have been waiting weeks or months to see the specialist, you want to make the most of the appointment. It may be helpful to bring another adult with you such as a relative or friend. If the baby is fussy or crying, it may be hard to concentrate or to have an in-depth conversation. Often there is a long wait in the office and naps and meals may be late. In addition, another person can help you ask questions and write down information.

4 ▶ HOME TREATMENT: POSITIONING

All of the caretaking of a reflux baby is centered on keeping her comfortable, keeping her upright and avoiding things that trigger symptoms. You are providing the home care treatment that your child needs to feel comfortable and to spit or vomit less. All this happens through two essential focus areas: positioning your baby and feeding your baby. *Positioning* means how you hold and support your child as you sooth, change, feed, play or lay your child down to sleep. *Feeding* is the routines you establish and the dietary changes you make as you and your child learn together what works and what doesn't work. Remember, all babies with GER and GERD benefit from the home treatments described in this section.

Studies have shown that keeping a baby upright after a feeding reduces vomiting, so you'll spend a lot of time doing just that! Your doctor will probably recommend various ways to include positioning as a home care treatment. Other reflux parents have found ingenious ways to position their baby, increasing comfort and reducing spitting and vomiting. Keep in mind that the goal of home care treatment is to reduce, not eliminate, spit up and vomiting. This may be very discouraging. Focus on the good news: reflux often improves steadily over time.

AVOID EXPOSURE TO SMOKE

Exposure to smoke has been proven to aggravate reflux, so do not allow anybody to smoke around your child. Ask your doctor for a prescription that says, "No smoking around the baby," and post it where all can see.

While keeping her upright is important, you don't want to forget that your baby still needs to both spend time in different positions and move around during the day. "Holding and playing," below, offer suggestions on how to accomplish this safely and happily!

Through trial and error, you have probably already figured out some "home care treatment" for your baby. There is an important reason why: your baby has communicated to you what she likes and needs. This chapter on "Positioning" and the next chapter, "Feeding," will give you many more ideas to try. Only your baby can tell you which ones help her.

Remember, there is no "one size fits all" home care treatment for reflux. You will need to try the strategies recommended by your doctor, the strategies presented here, and suggestions from other reflux parents. Take it slowly and try one new strategy at a time. If you have any doubts or concerns about a particular home care treatment, don't hesitate to discuss your concerns with your baby's doctor.

You may have heard about other babies taking medication for reflux symptoms. These medications, however, are only for babies with GERD, a less common and more serious condition. Babies with GER respond well to these straightforward home care techniques and do not need any other treatment. Whether your baby has GER or GERD, home care is an essential part of the treatment plan.

Soothing

Your baby is crying. It seems that no matter what you do, nothing can calm her. You and your baby are not alone. Once again, trial and error will show what works.

SOME IDEAS TO CONSIDER:

Swaddling: Swaddling is an age-old technique used to make your baby feel safe and secure. The arms are generally wrapped to prevent her from startling. If you try swaddling, use a light, stretchy blanket to firmly wrap your baby.

Movement: Swaying, gently rocking in a rocking chair or a car ride may sooth your crying baby.

> ## A Feeding Specialist Says...
>
> Many families find that certain types of music and sound can be extremely helpful to calm both the baby and the caretaker. Even something such as humming with the baby's back against your chest can work magic! The direction of movement is important, too. When the baby is held in an upright position, either across the shoulder or with the back against the adult's chest, the up-down vertical movement when you walk or gently jiggle is the same direction of movement they experienced in utero. This seems to be very calming and organizing for many babies.
>
> Suzanne Evans Morris, Ph.D., founder and director, New Visions

Distraction: Your baby may respond well to being distracted; it helps her think about something other than crying. Try taking her to another room or out to the park, changing her position, or playing classical music.

> ## A GER Mom says:
>
> I feel like I wear her all day and all night. I hardly have time to get a glass of water or answer the phone. I wish she could sit in ANY of her brand new baby equipment. It is just sitting here gathering dust while I hold her.

Loose Clothing: Make sure the diaper is loose and her waistbands aren't too tight or uncomfortable. Some parents routinely loosen the diaper after a feeding so it doesn't squeeze the stomach which can trigger reflux episodes.

Warm Bath: A warm bath may be distracting, and it might relax her. Get in with her and use this as play time or relaxation.

Take a Walk: Fresh air and bright light may make her sleepy. Or, she might be interested in having a look around.

Soothe the Caretaker: If you are tense and frustrated, your baby will be the first to know. Let someone else have a turn or put her in a stroller or seat for a few minutes while you take a break.

A GER Mom says:

My husband likes playing "airplane" with our son. Our son squeals with delight while perched on my husband's outstretched arms. It drives me crazy to watch him since I am so careful to move slowly and gently. Sometimes the "airplane" spits up but everyone enjoys this activity so much that it is worth it.

Holding and Playing
SOME IDEAS TO CONSIDER:

Minimize Bouncing and Jiggling: Train yourself to move slowly and avoid sudden movement, especially after a meal when her stomach is full.

Reduce the Pressure on her Stomach: She might prefer to be against your chest rather than over your shoulder. If she is high on your shoulder it can put too much pressure on her tummy.

Time to Adjust: When you try a positioning idea, do it for just a few minutes at a time and let her get used to it.

Try the Colic Hold : Lay her down with her tummy on your arm and her legs hanging down on each side of your arm. You can hold her with her head in the crook of your elbow or with her head in your hand. Figure out which feels safer for you and keep her head elevated a bit. Swaying while holding can help.

Consider this:

She loves looking at me if I lie down beside her or place her on a wedge.

Massage: A certified infant massage therapist can show you how to massage your baby. Parents report that infant massage decreases fussiness and reduces digestive discomfort.

34

Pass the Baby: Let dad, grandma or a neighbor take a turn holding the baby. This is hard work. You and your back need a break.

Tummy Time: With the "back to sleep" campaign, many babies spend more and more time on their backs during the first months of life. Because your baby spends additional time upright due to frequent vomiting, it may seem like there

---

Have Fun!

She laughs while looking at her cute little face in the mirror. It makes tummy time an enjoyable activity.

---

is no time to place her on her stomach.

You need to make "tummy time." Try placing her on her side or on her stomach throughout the day, even if it is just for a moment or two. She may cry and protest when you put her on her stomach because it is so new to her. Remember, if she is prone to spit up when she is on her stomach, try having tummy time before a meal!

Playing: Another idea is to ask dad to be in charge of play time. It may be very beneficial to everyone. Tummy time can be play time, too!

Sitting upright

Soothing, playing, and holding…yes, but sometimes your baby won't be or can't be in your arms. All parents reach for the latest and best independent "holder" for their child, and with an abundance of baby gear on the market today, we have many choices.

But what works for a baby with reflux? Below are a few ideas that this Reflux Mom and other parents found worked for them. Your baby is unique…so, it is trial and error once again. Rather than going out and buying an expensive item, it might be possible to get input from a veteran parent or borrow an item before purchasing it. Sharing information and experiences on baby equipment is a favorite topic on internet parent forums. Check them out!

SLINGS AND CARRIERS

Front Carrier: When you baby has some neck and back control, you may find that using a baby carrier is the best option to save your back and keep your baby comfortable. It may take a few tries to find the best style. This is a great way to keep her upright after a meal.

If you use a front carrier, you may have to adjust the carrier to keep your baby from slouching too much. She may feel more comfortable if the carrier comes all the way up to her armpits so the top edge is higher than her stomach and isn't putting pressure on the stomach.

Sling: Some babies with reflux love the semi-reclined position of a sling. You may find that she is more comfortable in the sling when turned onto her left side.

BABY SEATS, BOUNCERS AND SWINGS

There are a variety of baby seats and bouncers available in just about every baby store. A seat that keeps her legs straight rather than bent will decrease pressure on her stomach and provide the most comfort to her. It might be necessary to place a rolled up blanket or towel under the upper end of the seat, elevating her head. The reclining position can actually provoke reflux.

If your baby likes the infant seat, it may be tempting to keep her in it as she gets older. Be sure to follow the weight and age guidelines recommended by the manufacturer in order to ensure safety.

Your baby might enjoy sitting upright in a swing. Some babies like the motion of swinging while others become upset or vomit. Again...trial and error.

UPRIGHT SEATING

Once your baby has good head and trunk control and can almost sit up by herself, she might like an entertainment center/saucer or a high chair. It is important for her to have good control so she doesn't slide down or lean forward and put pressure on her stomach. A high chair can be a nice play surface for a baby who is very active and needs to stay in place a few minutes to digest a meal before resuming her busy schedule of crawling, climbing and spitting.

CAR SEATS

Car seats are designed to securely hold a baby during car rides. Sometimes, out of desperation, parents find that a car seat can do much more, offering a baby with reflux a comfortable place for play and sleep.

It might help to place a small receiving blanket in the base of the seat to decrease the sitting angle and lessen the pressure on her stomach.

If your baby cries while she is in the car seat, it is possible that the reclining position of the car seat is causing her to reflux. You might want to try a more upright model or you might just have to delay the long trip to grandma's house until she is feeling better. Traveling at night is one way to avoid a very long and loud car ride.

If your baby chokes or vomits a lot in the car seat, it might distract you so much that you drive dangerously. If at all possible, have another adult sit beside the baby.

Diaper Changing

If your baby cries or protests when you change her diaper, it may indicate that she is refluxing when she is placed on her back.

A GER Dad Says...

Whenever I placed him on his back for diaper changes, his little arms and legs would start to flail and he had a panicked look on his face. I bought a wedge for the changing table and he was a lot happier at diaper changing time!

Elevate the changing table: Parents often use a wedge to elevate one end of the changing table so their baby is never laying flat during diaper or clothing changes. As always, it is extremely important to use a safety strap and to stay beside your baby every moment she is on the changing table.

When to change: Parents often worry about changing their baby right after a feeding. Should you wait for 30 minutes so she can remain upright and digest her food? Will she stop fussing after a meal if she had a dry diaper on? You will need to use trial and error to decide what works best for her.

Lay her on her tummy: You can also try diapering your baby while she is lying on her tummy by rolling her from side to side. It takes practice. A few parents have even figured out how to keep their toddler completely upright during diaper changes – this involves two adults but may be worth the effort.

Sleep Positioning

This is the most difficult decision for reflux parents to make, largely because various guidelines may seem contradictory. Many doctors recommend, and many parents have found, that elevating the sleep surface so the head is higher than the body can reduce nighttime reflux episodes and help your baby or child sleep longer. However, the American Academy of Pediatrics does not endorse any wedge or sleeping device. The most important course of action is to discuss positioning with your child's doctor.

The American Academy of Pediatrics (AAP) recommends that all babies be placed on their backs to sleep. The AAP Guidelines used to state that babies with reflux were exempt from this recommendation. One of the oldest treatments for reflux was to have the baby sleep face down with her head elevated. However, new studies indicate the risk of Sudden Infant Death Syndrome or SIDS is greater for the average baby than the risk of choking. In 2005, the AAP dropped the exemption for babies with reflux and now insists that *all* babies sleep on their backs. There are a very small number of babies who tend to choke from reflux while laying flat on their backs. If you have seen your child choking while on her back, please have a long talk with your baby's doctor.

A WORD ABOUT SAFETY

You and your doctor will need to determine the best sleep position for your infant or child. The positioning devices described in this section are suggestions you can bring to your doctor at you next doctor's visit. Discuss your baby's particular needs and formulate your home treatment plan for positioning with the doctor. You attention should be given to:

Elevating the mattress: Check with the doctor *before* elevating your baby's mattress; if she recommends elevating her sleep surface, *then* use a wedge or any other positioning device. Remember, not all babies are the same and formulating a positioning treatment plan with your baby's doctor is step #1.

AMERICAN ACADEMY OF PEDIATRICS SLEEP POSITION RECOMMENDATIONS

The American Academy of Pediatrics (AAP) recommends that babies be placed on their backs, in a separate bed with a firm surface, in their parents' room. Babies should be dressed lightly so they don't overheat. The AAP has not tested or approved any of the sleeping devices described here. When considering their use, talk to your pediatrician on this home care treatment.

Making your own positioning device: Think you might make your own positioning device? Actually, it is not easier for you to make your own elevating device using things you have around the house. Don't let the seeming simplicity of wedges and hammocks lead you astray! With any modification to your baby's sleep surface, there is the potential for safety hazards due to getting caught or wedged in. With that in mind, review the options that other doctors and parents have found to be helpful elements in a home care treatment plan.

Raising the head of the crib may reduce reflux episodes and help your baby sleep better. There is some evidence that it is necessary to raise the sleep surface to approximately a 30 to 45 degree angle. Some parents find that even a slight incline in the sleep surface helps. If you use a steep angle, you will find your baby scoots down to the bottom of the bed and may get turned around. There are several commercially available wedges (see resource list) that combine a wedge with a strap or positioning device to keep your baby from sliding.

BED LIFTS

To raise one end of the crib or bed a few inches, bed lifts may be purchased from any bedding store. The crib may be far less stable and more prone to tipping over. Test the stability by rocking the crib. Remember that your baby will eventually be standing in the crib and trying to climb out. It should also be stable enough that a sibling or dog can't tip the crib over.

HAMMOCK

A reflux hammock is a special device that looks like an infant swing and keeps a baby positioned at an incline. The special construction keeps the baby from slipping down or turning on her tummy. Be aware: the US Consumer Product Safety Commission has recalled a different style of hammock that hangs inside a crib frame and has also banned the use of plain string hammocks because babies have suffocated in them or managed to put their heads over the edge.

CO-SLEEPING

Some parents find that the only way they can get any sleep is to bring the baby into their bed. The American Academy of Pediatrics does not advocate co-sleeping but if necessary, the AAP recommends an alternative product called a "co-sleeper." A commercially made co-sleeper is a three sided bassinet that fastens to the parents' bed. It keeps baby safe on her own sleep surface while keeping her close to you.

5 ►Home Care Treatment: Feeding Your Baby

If your baby is a "happy spitter," she is eating with ease...then promptly burps or burps up the entire feeding while smiling at you in her oh, so charming way! She doesn't experience any pain or discomfort from eating or spitting. She may grow just fine if she is able to keep down just enough food or if you re-feed after she has vomited. Doctors often are not concerned about this pattern and refer to it as a "laundry problem" rather than a "medical problem." Happy spitters don't normally need any medical treatment. However, some parents find that special feeding techniques may decrease the "laundry problem."

Whether your baby smiles or cries as she tosses her meal on the feeding bib, most parents have found feeding their baby with reflux to be the most challenging thing they have ever done. You will find yourself doing a great deal of experimenting to identify the right combination of foods and feeding techniques to help your baby. Don't lose sight of an important guideline in all this trying and testing: the best food for your baby is the food that causes the least amount of distress to her digestive system. As you move through this process, your pediatrician can be helpful in assuring that what your baby *will eat* is also what will help her grow and develop.

Breast is Best

With rare exceptions, breast milk is best for an infant with GER or GERD. Breast milk digests faster than formula which minimizes reflux. You may find that breastfeeding decreases your workload because it is available on demand. An added benefit is that when you nurse, hormones that help you relax are released, a real bonus when you are dealing with a fussy baby all day.

41

NURSING MOTHER'S DIET

In the past, mothers were told to stop eating "gassy" foods such as broccoli, cabbage and onions when they were nursing. Yet there is little evidence that eliminating these foods will reduce fussiness or other digestive symptoms. There is still some controversy about the need to eliminate foods from a nursing mother's diet. Some mothers are told to eliminate foods that are most likely to cause food allergies: milk, soy, tree nuts, peanuts, wheat and eggs.

> ### A GER Mom Says...
>
> After being on the elimination diet for two weeks I did notice that my son was a little better. I added back eggs and everything seemed ok. A week later my son was actually doing really well, so I decided to reintroduce soy. Immediately all of the symptoms came back - pulling off the breast, screaming, refusing to nurse, and general fussiness and unexplained screaming periods. After only 2 days of eating soy products, it has taken a full week to get my son back to "normal." Just in the last couple of days he's actually been happy when awake, he's sleeping better than ever, and just today he's finally back to nursing well with no fussing.

One way to determine if a food is causing a reaction is to try an elimination diet. A nursing mother follows a strict diet and gradually adds one food or food group back at a time. The baby is observed for signs of digestive distress, rashes or hives, indicating that a food is causing the symptoms.

If the baby has a known food allergy, the mother will need to eliminate the food from her diet. It may be very stressful to a nursing mother to eat a restricted diet since there isn't always time to read labels, shop carefully and prepare meals from scratch. In addition, it isn't always clear that eliminating foods from your diet has made a difference.

MAINTAINING YOUR SUPPLY

The quality of the breast milk is affected by your diet and a healthy lifestyle. If your diet is severely limited from a special diet or you are extremely stressed and sleepless, the quantity and quality of your milk may decrease. It is also important to stay hydrated to maintain your supply.

Deciding to Try Formula

Some mothers feel very disappointed when they can't nurse or nurse as long as they had planned. Even with a supportive family, or household help, it can be exhausting to stay on a special diet, take care of a baby night and day and get the nutrients you need. Even if you can only nurse for a little while, you are giving your baby important benefits.

> ### A GER Mom Says...
>
> I was so convinced my milk was bad for my baby that I switched to formula. Talk about jumping out of the frying pan into the fire! Now we are on the musical formula merry go round and he still vomits every day.

If you want to try formula for a few days, you can still maintain your milk supply. Simply pump your milk at regular intervals during the day and freeze it. If you find that she is just as unhappy with the formula as the breast milk, you have the option of going back to nursing or staying with bottle feeding.

If you have struggled with nursing for a while or chose not to nurse, bottle feeding may be the right choice. In the end,

> ### A GER Mom Says:
>
> I had already tried 3 formulas without success and the doctor suggested yet another one. The difference was like night and day. He was less fussy right from the first bottle and has gotten progressively better with time. We are now vomit free except for the occasional spit up! He can eat 6 ounces at a time and last night he slept 9 hours! He is so tremendously different-just so happy! My husband and I are both so relieved.

seeing your baby thrive, regardless of the diet is the sweetest sight.

Formula Options

The variety of infant formula options can be overwhelming. The advantages of formula include control over ingredients and elimination of possible allergens. An additional benefit of bottle feeding is that feeding and night waking duties can be shared with another caretaker.

All infant formulas sold in the United States are certified by the government to provide complete nutrition. You should not use products such as rice milk that do not contain adequate nutrition for infants and are not officially certified as baby formulas. All of the infant formulas on the market claim different benefits and ingredients to promote growth and

---

Formula Categories

Milk Based: contains whole dairy proteins.
  - Lactose Free Formula: milk based formula with no milk sugar.
  - Formula with added rice thickener.

Soy Based: contains whole soy proteins.

Partly Hydrolyzed Formula: proteins are partly broken down; often marketed as "gentler."
  - Soy based
  - Whey based
  - Casein based

Extensively Hydrolyzed: proteins are well broken down; marketed as "hypoallergenic," but some babies still react.
  - Soy based
  - Whey based
  - Casein based

Amino Acid Formula: No proteins or partial proteins at all. Lowest chance of allergic reactions although rare reactions do occur.

---

development. The bottom line is all formulas strive to achieve what breast milk does.

You and your doctor will consider different formulas as a treatment because some babies seem to digest certain kinds of formula better than others. You may have noticed that formulas are milk or soy based, while others are lactose free, pre-digested or hypoallergenic. Some infant formula is even thickened. There is really no one perfect formula for all babies with reflux. Again…trial and error.

Babies with Milk Soy Protein Intolerance (MSPI) and some children with allergies react to proteins of any sort and must use amino acid formulas. Amino acids are the building blocks

---

MONEY SAVING TIPS WHEN BUYING FORMULA

- If you have to buy formula, you know the prices range from expensive to really extraordinarily expensive so **buy the smallest amount** possible at first.
- **Check your medical insurance** to see if they pay for special formula. It may be called Medical Formula or Medical Food and require a prescription or a letter from the doctor.
- **Ask for samples** of thickeners and formula from your doctor or pharmacist. Thickeners come in a large canister and cannot be returned.
- **Ask the doctor for coupons** for formula.

---

of proteins. When a person eats proteins, they are broken down into amino acids which are then used to build new proteins like muscles.

Keep in mind that amino acid based formula is very expensive and should be used under the direction of a physician. Insurance may cover the cost but will often deny coverage for these expensive formulas. It is possible you will need to contact the insurance company for authorization or ask the doctor to write a letter.

FINDING THE RIGHT FORMULA

Parents and doctors may find that they need to try more than one formula before finding one that is a good match for the baby. Parents often need to monitor the baby and convey observations to the doctor about tolerance of the formula. Clues that a formula may not be a good match for your baby are: constipation, increased fussiness, vomiting, skin rash, blood in the stool or diaper rash.

FOOD ALLERGIES AND INTOLERANCES

It is possible for a baby or child to have an allergy or intolerance to almost any food. Foods that cause allergies may present with an immediate reaction such as a skin rash, hives or breathing difficulties. The most common food allergies are

---

A GER Mom's Decision...

I chose not to introduce solids until 6 months. It was well after a year when I started to introduce wheat, egg whites, corn, tomato, as well as dairy and soy. Papaya was an early hit, and that is really good for digestion.

---

milk, fish, shellfish, nuts, peanuts, wheat, soy and eggs. Lactose and milk soy protein are the most commonly found food intolerances in infants.

Tips for Feeding Your Baby

Ok, this is where everything comes together—all your discussions with the pediatrician about breast vs. formula, working out how best to breast feed or what formula to use. Now, you need to figure out the best way to feed *your* baby. Again, your baby is unique...so it's...yes, trial and error!

The first step to success is **positioning your baby** on the breast to ensure a good latch on. This will minimize air intake with feedings and reduce digestive discomfort from trapped air in the stomach.

Remember, both you and your baby need to **work together** to make nursing successful. Often too much blame is placed on the mother for nursing failure. We don't want to forget that the baby needs to have a coordinated suck and a good seal on the nipple to stimulate the milk and take in nourishment.

Also, you want to keep in mind that successful feeding is not only about volume, it is about the **nutritional content** your baby gets from your breast milk. For instance, if your baby gets the foremilk, which is high in lactose and low fat, but doesn't get the high fat, high calorie hind milk, it can result in weight issues, fussiness and gassy, smelly bowel movements.

One common cause of **choking, gagging or refusing the breast** is an overactive let-down, where the milk comes too fast for your baby to handle.

Also, a baby who is in pain may **fight the breast**. It may be difficult to nurse her, but not impossible. For example, offering only one breast at each feeding is a common strategy for babies with reflux.

You can get help with this and other nursing issues from a lactation specialist or a La Leche leader who will assist you with specific difficulties.

SMALL, FREQUENT FEEDING

It may be necessary to feed small, frequent meals so that your baby is never too full and never too hungry. While baby books may tell you that it is important to get baby on a schedule and wait 3-4 hours between feeding, that advice may not apply to a baby with reflux. If she waits too long between feedings, she may be frantic and suck air in her effort to eat quickly and relieve the pain of hunger. She may be inclined to over feed and get too full. On the other hand, if you try to get her to finish the last few ounces in her bottle or take the other breast, she may eat more than her stomach needs at the moment.

By letting her nibble a bit here, a bit there, she is putting less pressure on her stomach and learning to regulate her intake. She can sense when she needs to eat and start to signal you when she needs more. You need to work with her and read her signals - is she rooting for your breast or making a little fussing sound? She may be communicating to you that she is ready for a little snack. Remember, she said "little snack," not a "three course meal!"

The other babies (you know…the ones without reflux) in your new moms group may have learned to eat enough during the day that they sleep peacefully all night. Your baby may be eating less during the day so that night feedings are necessary to get caught up on calories. You may have heard others tell you that she is too old to be waking up at night and you need to "teach" her to stop bothering you at night. Don't feel anxious; reflux babies feed differently. When she is able to eat a bigger meal without distress, you can certainly encourage her to sleep at that point. Perhaps you can reduce one night feeding at a time until she is able to sleep all night. The earlier section on "Sleeping" has more ideas on helping to make this happen.

MINIMIZE AIR INTAKE WITH FEEDING

Regardless of whether you are nursing or bottle feeding, it is important to ensure a good latch so that baby's lips are sealed around the bottle or breast. You can test whether she has a good seal by gently pulling back the nipple to see if she is able to keep her mouth around the bottle. If the bottle comes out of her mouth easily or she is a noisy eater, she may not have a good latch and seal.

A good seal will decrease the intake of air with each suck minimizing bloating and discomfort. Your baby may think she is full when she is just full of air. Crying can also increase air intake. Frequent burping may be necessary to release the trapped air.

Some types of baby bottles are designed to decrease air intake during drinking. If it looks like your baby has a good seal on the bottle and she is still ingesting too much air, you may want to try a different bottle or nipple.

When she is done eating, burping may relieve stomach pressure and release trapped air. On the other hand, burping may bring up acid and she won't want to finish eating.

RATE AND FLOW

It may be important to adjust the rate and flow of the milk supply. If the milk is coming out too fast, your baby may take big gulps of milk to try to keep up, ingesting air at the same time. If the rate is too slow, she may tire and give up on eating. For breastfeeding, it may be necessary to express a bit of milk first if the let down produces a gush of milk, causing choking and gasping.

If you are bottle feeding, the nipple on a bottle may be switched to regulate the rate and flow of milk. Some parents report that they have tried several types of bottles and nipples before finding one that is just right for their little one.

THICKENING FORMULA AND BREAST MILK

It is thought that thickened liquids stay in the stomach better and may decrease vomiting. This recommendation is somewhat controversial. While studies have shown that thickening liquids reduces vomiting, it does not reduce reflux episodes. So the thickened formula can still come up, but perhaps not so far. There is also some concern that cereal and other thickeners reduce the intake of nutrient rich formula or breast milk and adds too much "filler." The baby may gain weight from the extra calories but may have a decreased intake of vital nutrients. Some babies become constipated from rice cereal and other thickeners. There is also concern that adding food (including thickeners) to an infant's diet too soon may increase susceptibility to the development of allergies. It is important to monitor your baby closely if you choose to thicken feeds. If thickened feeds decrease vomiting

> ### *Jan Says...*
>
> While it may be tempting to feed her in a car seat or bouncy chair, it is better to hold her in your arms. A car seat is likely to bend her little body so there is too much pressure on her stomach. In addition, she needs to be close to you so she can see you and feel the warmth of your body. Even if it hurts to eat, she needs to know that you are there for her.

and help your baby to grow without the need for medication, this may be the best way to feed your baby.

Breast milk or formula may be thickened with rice cereal or another thickener such as oatmeal, barley or potato flakes. Read the labels carefully to make sure the thickener does not have any added ingredients. Doctors often recommend adding one tablespoon of thickener such as rice cereal per ounce of liquid. Thickened liquids will be the consistency of tomato sauce. You can purchase special X and Y cut nipples for feeding thickened liquids.

It is difficult to thicken breast milk because the enzymes in the milk will break up the thickener causing the milk to thin out rapidly. It is best to thicken breast milk just before feeding or just thicken 1-2 ounces at a time. When your baby gets old enough to eat cereal, try giving her a few spoonfuls before nursing.

POSITIONING

Positioning your baby for feeding is also very important. A very young baby may need to be wrapped securely in a blanket to minimize movement and help her relax. You may have seen the nurse swaddle your baby in the hospital.

Some babies need to be held upright while feeding. It may help to keep her legs straight so there is less pressure on her stomach. Curling her up into a little ball may place pressure on her stomach and literally squeeze the food right out. The result may be vomiting of her entire meal. Finding the right position may feel very awkward for both of you. Ask a nurse or lactation specialist to help you find a comfortable position that allows your baby to be upright.

After a meal, your baby may need to be held in an upright position for up to 30 minutes to allow her to digest her meal and minimize vomiting. Some parents sit in a comfortable chair with their baby held up to their shoulder. Others use an infant carrier or an infant seat to keep her semi-reclined.

PART 2 ▶ GERD

6 ▶ GASTROESOPHAGEAL REFLUX DISEASE: GERD

Gastroesophageal Reflux Disease (GERD) refers to an abnormal pattern of reflux characterized by frequent, painful reflux episodes that last longer than those experienced by babies with GER. There is increasing evidence that GERD is a common chronic condition of childhood. A baby or child with GERD may experience discomfort which interferes significantly with feeding, sleep and daily activities that become the underlying cause for immediate and future health issues. GERD is a disease caused by an abnormal pattern of daily reflux events. The constant backwashing of stomach acid and partially digested food on the sensitive lining of the esophagus leads to irritation. Over time, the irritation leads to complications such as esophageal injury, respiratory symptoms and poor growth.

Characteristics of GERD

So what does a baby or child with GERD look like? Most

A GERD Mom Says:

When I took him in for his 4 week checkup, I mentioned to the doctor that he seemed to be crying more and more often especially at night. I asked the doctor if he could have nightmares or night terrors at his age because he would sleep for about an hour and then wake up screaming and did this all night. We soon learned that it was reflux and not night terrors that was causing the night waking.

---

parents and doctors would describe the typical characteristics as fussiness or irritability ranging from mild to severe. It is common for a baby or toddler with GERD to have some significant difficulties with eating and sleeping. A baby with GERD is definitely *not* a "happy spitter."

53

What really separates GERD from GER is the irritation or damage caused by the acid. It is likely you as a parent will notice the characteristics of GERD that affect your baby the most; the doctor will carefully assess the problems or complications caused by the acid such as respiratory, growth and irritation/damage to the esophagus.

Please remember that only a doctor can diagnose *Gastroesophageal Reflux Disease*. The information presented in this chapter is not a substitute for medical advice. It is intended to help you proceed more confidently as your baby's advocate and care giver. It will guide you in documenting your child's symptoms, helping you bring your observations and concerns to a doctor for an accurate diagnosis.

FROM FUSSY TO INCONSOLABLE

The pain from reflux may make your baby fussy in a variety of ways. She may cry endlessly no matter what you try: holding, feeding or driving in the car. On the other hand,

Jan Says...

My baby wanted to be held constantly and nothing soothed her. It was impossible to get anything done. Through a combination of aggressive medical treatment and helping her learn ways to sooth herself, she learned to play for a few minutes at a time.

◆

Sad Sarah

Sarah was a fussy infant and became a clingy and grumpy toddler. Who could blame her? She never slept more than an hour or two at night without waking up. I could hear her gulping hard and coughing. If I let her cry it out, she would vomit all over the crib.

she may be happy most of the time with sudden outbursts of crying or wake up from a deep sleep and cry out.

Remember, not all crying and pain is from reflux. Colic, constipation and many other medical conditions need to be considered when evaluating a baby who is in pain (return to

Section 1 for an in-depth discussion of these medical conditions).

Poor sleep and chronic discomfort can cause your little one to be whiny or clingy. Some toddlers may become hyperactive, angry or aggressive.

Fussiness: Some babies with reflux are fussy and irritable with short, fleeting periods of happy alertness. Toddlers may express pain by being extra clingy or fussy with a short frustration tolerance. They are notoriously bad at being able to identify the source of their discomfort and may lash out or switch moods suddenly.

Inconsolable crying: It is painful to be in the same room with a baby who will not stop shrieking, arching her back, clawing and flailing. The piercing pain of a baby in this level of distress can be very upsetting to a caretaker. Some babies with

---

A GERD Mom's Experience...

She cried so hard and so long that she was hoarse. Her face was red and she was covered in sweat. I was also in tears and completely exhausted. Nothing helped. My husband and I took turns holding her, rocking her, changing her diaper, feeding her—we even gave her a bath. She just would not calm down.

◆

After crying most of the day my neighbor took the baby to her house. I was exhausted and went right to bed. When I opened my window, I could hear her screaming from next door.

---

severe pain from reflux have been known to cry for hours.

Arching Back: Some babies will respond to the pain experienced during eating or reflux episodes by arching their back. Even though babies may not be very mobile, they can use their strong back muscles to pull away from the breast or bottle. You may notice arching most during mealtime as you both change positions, struggling to find a comfortable position. It may feel like you are baby wrestling rather than providing nourishment. See Sandifer's Syndrome.

POOR EATING AND SLEEPING

Most infants and children with GERD experience mild to severe difficulties with eating and sleeping. You may recognize some of these behaviors.

Vomiting: it is not uncommon for a baby with GERD to vomit during or after a feeding. Parents report a variety of patterns. Some babies vomit as soon as the formula or breast milk enters the stomach while others vomit just after a feeding. While a little bit of spit up or vomiting is to be expected, it is worrisome when a baby vomits an entire meal over and over again.

Vomiting usually slows down or stops altogether in the first year. However, some toddlers and children vomit, especially after a large meal or engaging in physical activity right after eating. Parents also report that toddlers and older children with GERD vomit more easily when ill or in the car.

> *A GERD Mom Says...*
>
> He had to be coaxed to drink a 4 ounce bottle. As soon as he was finished, he would vomit half of it right up. We kept a very close eye on our baby's weight. The pediatrician has us bring him in every other week for weight checks because he had fallen to the fifth percentile. She was concerned that he didn't have enough weight to spare if he got a fever and couldn't eat for a few days. We really had to work hard to nudge his weight back up to 5-10th percentile.

Poor eating, gagging and choking: While it is fairly common for babies to occasionally choke, a baby with reflux may do this at every meal. It may seem that she can't settle into a good feeding pattern and that you both have to start and stop frequently. If your baby experiences breathing problems during a choking episode, call 911 immediately.

Drooling: Immediately after a reflux event, the saliva glands may produce large amounts of saliva to help wash any acid out of the esophagus. You may notice your baby drools a lot even if she is not teething. This is called *water brash* or *hypersalivation*.

Silent reflux occurs when food and stomach contents enter the esophagus but are not expelled in the form of vomiting. The medical term is *occult reflux*: silent or hidden reflux. Silent reflux can be very painful to an infant or child. While an episode of vomiting may cause momentary discomfort, silent reflux can cause constant irritation from stomach acid on the delicate lining of the esophagus, traveling as high as the throat. On examination the doctor will sometimes notice that the throat is red. A baby may have a pained look, grimacing, crying out or hard swallowing. You may also hear grunting, choking, throat clearing or coughing during or after a meal.

> ### A GERD Mom Says...
>
> I thought the reflux was getting better because she stopped vomiting at 6 months of age. Then I realized her symptoms had changed and now she had silent reflux.

While spit up and vomiting are common signs of infant reflux, older babies and children are more likely to have silent reflux.

There is some concern that silent reflux may be under diagnosed and treated. Without an obvious symptom such as spit up or vomiting, it may be less obvious that there is a problem. In addition, the constant irritation to the esophagus may cause more long term problems.

Bad breath: Bad smelling breath will sometimes accompany other symptoms as a sign of reflux.

> ### Madison's Story
>
> Madison fussed and cried non stop and was the world's worse sleeper. People always say, "I slept like a baby. " Well, Madison would only sleep for 20-30 minutes at a time after she had exhausted herself from shrieking. Even when she was a newborn, she barely napped all day long.

Poor sleep: Many babies with reflux are such poor sleepers that there is a whole chapter devoted to this subject. Some have difficulty falling asleep and staying asleep; most lose sleep or do not sleep deeply, not falling asleep until they are utterly exhausted.

What happens is that during sleep, a combination of relaxed muscles (including the stomach muscles) and a reclined sleeping position allows acid to escape from the stomach, burning the esophagus and throat. Your child will wake up, scream or cry...and we come full circle to fussiness and inconsolable crying.

Complications from GERD

When you go to the doctor, your description—in great detail—of your child's experience, such as poor sleep, non-stop crying or consistently vomiting a meal, will signal the doctor that further investigation is needed. The details and documentation of your child's distress will help the doctor assess the severity of the problem. The doctor will also be looking at the possible complications or consequences of GERD. It helps to have a general knowledge of these potential problems and be prepared with your questions. These common complications associated with GERD are presented here. As you read, keep in mind that your doctor makes the diagnosis; you provide the accurate data.

GROWTH ISSUES

Reflux can have a big impact on growth. Frequent vomiting and/or poor feeding can lead to a pattern of slow growth or weight loss. The doctor monitors growth frequently during the course of well baby check ups. Slow growth is very worrisome to both you and your doctor but, in

Baby Alex's Story

Baby Alex choked and vomited from his first feeding in the hospital. The doctor told us to bring him in for extra office visit and gave us a long list of home care instructions. We took him home and did the best we could to comfort him and keep the formula down. At two weeks of age, the doctor said he was losing weight.

and of itself, it is not cause for panic. It does require your full attention and patience as you work to find the best, if not perfect, way your baby will accept and keep down what she eats. See "Practical Tips for Doctor Visits" in Section 1.

Underweight: If a worrisome pattern of slow weight gain develops, the doctor may ask you to bring your baby in more frequently for weight checks. Poor weight gain can be a sign that something is wrong and weight loss of more than a few ounces should be investigated right away. Gaining the right amount of weight is very important in helping your child grow and stay healthy. See "Failure to Thrive," below.

Overweight: Some babies with reflux grow just fine or even become quite over weight. Amazingly, yes your baby can overeat! She may have learned that it feels better to have a sip of milk to push the acid back down. From her point of view, she is trying to "fix" the reflux. It is also important to watch that she doesn't get her stomach overly full because over eating can aggravate reflux too.

BREATHING PROBLEMS

Little babies have little airways, so their breathing tends to sound loud and even congested at times. A baby with reflux may cough and gag during and after a meal if the meal she just ate is being refluxed back up again and aggravating her airway.

> ### Rebecca's Story
>
> Rebecca nursed non stop and gained weight steadily. Actually, she was the picture of health on the outside. Inside, silent reflux made her throat and esophagus red and irritated. The smallest cold turned into pneumonia and eventually scarred her lungs. The doctor said the reflux was causing her to aspirate.

There is some evidence that a baby with GERD may be more likely to have respiratory illnesses such as a cold or an upper airway infection because of fluid pooling in the sinuses and the lungs. GERD may also lead to aspiration of acid and stomach contents into the lungs causing irritation or infection.

If acid or acid vapors get all the way into the lungs, it can cause more serious complications such as pneumonia or bronchitis. If it weren't hard enough to know when to call the doctor with your child without reflux, this adds new tension and uncertainty about making that call. With reflux, don't hesitate. If your child with reflux develops a severe cough, call your doctor.

If the voice box becomes swollen, your child may get croup with a distinctive barking type cough caused by swollen vocal cords or *stridor* with a noisy inhalation. You know your child: if your experience tells you there may be a problem, check it out with the doctor.

At the worst, if your baby's face, lips and fingernails turn blue or dusky or pale grey, call the doctor or 911 immediately.

Jan Says...

I wrote an article for *Allergy and Asthma Today* called, "Noisy Asthma, Silent Reflux." It tells the story of my daughter Rebecca who coughed and wheezed loudly, but rarely vomited or showed obvious signs of reflux. It took quite a bit of effort to sort out the cause and effect. Once she was aggressively treated for both asthma and reflux, her lungs cleared and she felt much better.

Always, if your baby is having trouble breathing or stops breathing, call 911 immediately.

It is important to remember that not all children with reflux develop breathing problems. Nevertheless, as your child's advocate, you need to know that it is possible. Your job is to be alert to signs of trouble and not to hesitate to report any worrisome symptoms to your doctor. Let your doctor make the diagnosis.

Asthma: Many children with asthma also have reflux. Asthma is a constriction of the tubes in the lungs that makes it hard to exhale fully. It may cause a squeaky noise (wheezing), bouts of coughing, shortness of breath or a lack of energy.

There is some controversy about the connection between reflux and asthma. Reflux episodes may result from breathing hard due to asthma. As the chest is moving, the food in the stomach can be forced upward into the esophagus. In some people—infants, older children and adults—asthma and reflux symptoms may be caused by allergies. New research shows that a patient with reflux may develop asthma because the esophagus senses acid headed upward and "warns" the respiratory system to constrict to prevent acid from getting into the lungs. Even acid vapors and droplets in the esophagus are enough to provoke this response in some people.

Apnea and ALTE: *Apnea* refers to pauses in breathing– usually lasting more than 20 seconds. The traditional definition of apnea is a baby who sleeps so deeply, her brain forgets to keep the breathing at an even rate. An "Apparent Life Threatening Event" or *ALTE* is a prolonged apnea event. There is some evidence that reflux causes some apnea and ALTE, but more research is needed.

Any type of breathing problem, apnea event or ALTE needs to be evaluated by a medical doctor. Do not try to evaluate the severity of the problem yourself. Call 911 immediately. Even if your baby starts breathing again and seems fine, don't assume everything is fine. It is vital to have a complete medical evaluation and determine the cause of the breathing problems. An accurate evaluation by the doctor begins with a thorough description of the event. So, while you're doing everything else, let a part of your brain document all the details of what happened.

> ### A Parent Experience...
>
> It was the longest moment of my life. She started choking and then she just went limp. I turned her over and patted her back. She started breathing but she was pale and weak. Something was terribly wrong. I was so scared I could hardly dial the phone to call 911.

"Awake apnea": This occurs when, during a reflux episode, the body tries to protect the airway by shutting the vocal cords. This closes the airway. Occasionally, the vocal cords stay locked shut after the reflux is cleared. This is called a *laryngospasm* and is the main cause of "awake apnea" spells.

Even if your baby does not have a true apnea event, some babies have been known to have brief pauses in breathing, a pale or grey look to their face or blue lips. Again, these are worrisome signs of distress. Report this occurrence to the doctor immediately.

> ### *Hayley...*
>
> At 5 months of age, Hayley had a cough and a stuffy nose. I noticed that her lips were turning blue when I nursed her but her color returned to normal when she stopped nursing. I called the doctor right away and I was told to bring her in. Of course when I got there, her color was normal. The doctor said I did the right thing by bringing her in.

DAMAGE

Hoarseness: Babies and children with acid damage to the voice box may have a hoarse or very deep sounding voice. You may be wondering how a baby can have a hoarse voice when they cannot even talk. Parents of a child with reflux have said that the crying and fussing sound hoarse, like the baby has a sore throat.

> ### *A GERD Mom Says...*
>
> I was sure she had esophagitis or an ulcer. Her long bouts of crying had to be from more than just reflux, but the tests didn't show any damage to her esophagus.

Esophageal Damage: It is often surprising to parents that most infants do not have esophageal injury, even a baby who shrieks with pain for hours on end. Though we hear a lot about esophageal damage in adults, it is not common in children. When exposed to acid, your baby's esophagus becomes red and swollen (esophagitis). *Esophageal damage* occurs on those rare cases where the lining of the esophagus develops raw spots called ulcers. If the ulcers bleed, the child may vomit blood or pass dark, tarry stools (looks like coffee grounds and smells terrible). In rare cases, children can become anemic from losing too much blood.

Strictures, a webbed type of scar tissue, may form when esophageal damage heals. The strictures may partially block the esophagus causing food to get stuck on the way down to the stomach.

If the esophagus is constantly being bathed with acid, the cells lining the esophagus may start to change and become more like stomach lining cells which are not damaged by stomach acid. This is the clever way the body protects the esophagus, by making the esophagus lining less delicate. The danger is when, after many years of refluxing, these hybrid stomach/esophagus cells grow out of control. The term for the half stomach/half esophageal cells is Barrett's Esophagus or pre-cancer. Fortunately, Barrett's Esophagus is very rare in infants and children.

Tooth enamel erosion: The enamel on the surfaces of the teeth may be eroded and damaged from exposure to refluxed acid and stomach contents. Other signs that your baby's teeth are at risk for damage include bad breath and constant drooling. It is important to keep a close eye on your baby's teeth and to make your baby's dentist an early member of your "Team Reflux".

ILLNESS AND CHRONIC PROBLEMS

Ear and sinus infections: When an adult refluxes, the back of the mouth (soft palate) rises to block acid from squeezing up into the nose and sinuses. In babies, the soft palate may not block the acid and she may vomit out of her nose. If the acid gets into the sinuses, it can remove the mucus that helps defend her from viruses.

During infancy, the Eustachian tube is more horizontal than in older children and adults. As a result, it is easy for formula and reflux to move from the back of the throat into the middle ear. There is some evidence that acid may cause burning ear pain or an ear infection. As a result, some ear, nose and throat doctors believe there is an association between reflux and ear infections.

Sandifer's Syndrome: *Sandifer's Syndrome* is the term used to describe spastic, arching body movements that babies make when they are in pain. Other terms for this condition include *temporary torticollis* (head tilting to one side) and *secondary dystonia* (a lack of normal muscle control). Sometimes, the movements associated with Sandifer's Syndrome look like seizures so a doctor may refer a baby to a neurologist or the Emergency Room for evaluation. If testing rules out actual seizures, additional treatments to lessen pain from reflux may be recommended.

Dysphagia: *Dysphagia* is a medical term for a "swallowing problem." A baby with dysphagia may experience coughing and gagging during meals due to difficulty coordinating sucking, breathing and swallowing. Over time, a baby or toddler with dysphagia may become resistant to trying new textures and foods.

Unusual Symptoms

A few children with gastroesophageal reflux disease seem to have significant medical complications. This small group of children may not respond to standard treatments, may have an unusually severe form of GERD and/or may have other medical conditions. The bottom line is your child is just not getting better despite a medicine cabinet full of medications and endless trips to the doctor and pharmacy. It may seem like you spend all of your time going to appointments. In this situation, parents and physicians may consider new tests and treatments or even consult with other specialists. It can be very frustrating to everyone.

You may find yourself doing your own networking and research. It can get to the point where you are bringing research studies to the doctor's appointment or asking about rare diseases or new tests that are only available in some research clinic across the country.

If you are raising a child with unusual symptoms, you will need to find a doctor who is willing to think out of the box and help you manage the sometimes complicated assortment of specialists, tests and treatments that are needed. It can be helpful to talk with a support organization and network with other parents who have struggled to find the combination of treatments to help children with complicated medical needs.

ZEBRA HUNTING

In medical school, the saying goes, "If you hear hoof beats, think horses. There are many horses but few zebras." Loosely translated, it means, before considering an exotic or rare illness, don't overlook a common diagnosis. So a "zebra" in medical slang is a rare or unusual medical problem. Doctors are cautioned not to immediately consider a rare condition before looking at the possibility of a common medical problem. So when is it time to move on, to look at the rare possibilities?

Parents of refluxers often get scolded by the doctor for reading about rare complications and related conditions of GERD, then assuming the worst. But sometimes Dr. Mom is

correct. As you nudge Team Reflux on, avoid coming across to the doctor as bossy or overbearing. Listen to your doctor's point of view and assessment of the symptoms you are worried about. Open dialogue is always in the best interest of your child.

Gastroesophageal Reflux Disease (GERD) may be triggered by another condition such as an allergy or your child may have GERD and another health condition. You and your doctor may consider other diseases that have look alike symptoms if your child does not respond to typical treatments or seems to have multiple symptoms or odd symptoms. We'll start with the more common conditions:

Common Conditions Associated with GERD

Fructose Intolerance	**Milk/Soy Protein Intolerance**
Lactose Intolerance	**Gastroparesis/delayed gastric emptying**

If "horses" are scarce you and your doctor may start looking for some "zebras." Here are the rare conditions only a few parents are going to see on the horizon:

Rare Conditions Associated with GERD

Achalasia	Laryngospasm
Alkaline Reflux	Laryngomalacia
Autonomic Dysfunction	Metabolic Diseases
Celiac Disease / Gluten	Mitochondrial Disorders
Intolerance	Orthostatic Tachycardia
Cyclic Vomiting Syndrome	Postural Orthostatic
Cystic Fibrosis	Tacycardia
Dysphagia	(POTS)
Eosinophilic Diseases	Pyloric Stenosis / Pyloric
Esophageal Stenosis	Spams
Esophageal Atresia	Tracheo-Esophageal
Helicobactor Pylori	Fistula

Developmental Issues

Developmental delay is a term used when milestones such as language, play, and movement are reached later than expected. It is normal for infants and children to develop skills at different rates. However, an infant or child with GERD may have developmental delays for a variety of reasons associated with reflux. Below are descriptions of delays experienced by babies or children with GERD. As you observe your child and report developmental delays to your pediatrician, you can discuss what action, if any, is required.

MOTOR DELAY

There is a great deal of variability in the rate children learn to use large muscles for sitting, pulling to stand and walking. Some babies have low muscle tone (hypotonia) or high muscle tone (hypertonia). The muscle tone may affect the ability to learn motor skills such as crawling or walking and small muscle skills like chewing and swallowing. For instance, low muscle tone can cause poor motility and difficulty learning to eat solids. If your infant has been ill from GERD she might

---

How a GERD Mom Feels...

I find myself holding her as if I am carrying a piece of priceless china. I am so worried about a sudden movement that will cause her to vomit. After a bottle, I hold her over my shoulder and hope that the food stays down.

---

have missed opportunities to learn skills as quickly as other babies. Your baby may have been held much more than a baby without reflux to reduce crying and allow a favorable position for digestion. You wouldn't dare dance around the living room with your infant to the beat of a favorite tune. Next to getting the food in, the most important task was KEEPING it in!!

While the increased holding and positioning have been successful as a form of treatment, it may have also led to reduced movement opportunities. You may have noticed that your baby did not sit up or crawl/walk as quickly as other babies. Your baby may have a bald patch on the back of her head from sitting upright in the baby carrier to digest. It is always a good idea to report your concerns about motor skills development to the doctor. In addition, it might be a good idea to help her to move and try new positions as her digestive system allows.

The fact that she is not sitting up or crawling on the same timetable as other babies may be yet another opportunity to blame yourself for your parenting decisions. Remember, you did the best you could. Most likely, your baby will be just fine and the story will have a happy ending!

SPEECH DELAY

A baby with GERD may have a few obstacles in her path to developing speech. A baby who is crying in pain 24/7 may miss out on play experiences that help develop sounds used for communication. Some of the muscles used for eating are also used for speech and the lack of practice can slow sound and speech development a bit.

DELAYED FEEDING SKILLS

Feeding skills may be delayed due to a variety of reasons including: inability to eat a variety of foods due to an oral motor issue, lack of readiness or lack of experience. While all of your friends were feeding their babies jar after jar of baby food, you were trying to coax your baby to just take a spoonful. In most cases, a slow start to feeding will not lead to long term feeding issues. With opportunities to try new foods and utensils, she will develop new feeding skills at her own pace.

WHEN TO SEEK HELP

During well baby check ups, it is likely that your doctor will ask you questions about development. Your doctor may be able to perform a simple test of skills (called a screening) in the office. Based on this information, your doctor can determine if skills are developing at the expected pace. If your doctor determines that further testing is needed, he/she may make a referral for a more in depth developmental screening.

A Child Find or Early Intervention program is available in most communities and offers free developmental screening and testing for children from birth to age 5 years. You will be given a written report that describes the testing and any recommended treatments.

Reflux in Special Populations

Gastroesophageal Reflux Disease is extremely common in children with special needs. A child with autism, neurological

> ## *A GERD Mom Says...*
>
> My child has multiple medical and development issues and is confined to a wheelchair. He needs help with eating, dressing, bathing and mobility. However, the hardest thing for me is to deal with his reflux; it wakes him up at night, it makes him irritable and it makes it hard to feed him.

and muscle tone issues, Down syndrome or prematurity is more likely to be affected. A child with special needs may have a multitude of developmental, behavioral and medical issues so it can be hard to sort out all of the symptoms. Parents report that the reflux is often overlooked and under-diagnosed when there are other issues.

For many children with special needs, there are numerous obstacles to good eating and nutrition. Problems with sensory processing and swallowing may lead to poor intake, limited acceptance of textures and flavors and aspiration during feeding. Poor muscle tone and some medications such as seizure medication may increase reflux episodes leading to digestive issues and discomfort. It can be very difficult and time consuming to feed a child with special needs and ensure that enough nutrients and fluids are consumed to maintain health.

PREMATURITY

Gastroesophageal Reflux Disease is extremely common in babies born early or prematurely. A baby born prematurely may have feeding and digestive issues due to an immature neurological system, medications, breathing issues and an immature digestive system. A premature baby may need special feeding assistance from an occupational therapist, speech language pathologist and dietician.

DOWN SYNDROME

About 50-70% of children with Down syndrome have reflux symptoms. Low muscle tone can cause the muscles of the esophagus and stomach (Lower Esophageal Sphincter) to open more easily, allowing acid to reflux upward into the esophagus. Many children with Down syndrome have difficulty with feeding since the low muscle tone also affects sucking and swallowing. Your child may need more time and patience to progress to textured food and table food. It is important to look for non verbal cues from your child to determine if she is in pain or having trouble managing the texture or flavor of a new food. It can be scary to choke on food and so it is important to go slowly when starting a new way of eating.

A GERD Mom Says...

My son with autism developed intense, frequent temper tantrums at age 3. His doctor prescribed an antidepressant to control his outbursts. I felt really uncomfortable about this and called his pediatric gastroenterologist because he still had mild reflux symptoms after stopping his reflux medication a few months ago. It was decided to try a dose of reflux medication for two weeks to see if this would help the reflux and the behavior. I was amazed to see him transform almost immediately. He still had occasional tantrums but he slept and ate better and best of all, he said 3 new words.

Autism

Gastroesophageal reflux is extremely common in children with autism. However, it may be difficult to sort out the symptoms since many children with autism also have extreme food preferences (only eat green food, only eat crunchy food), as well as sensory processing issues. In addition, communication may be significantly affected, leading to poor communication of wants and needs (hunger, pain, request food, end a meal). You may find that it takes a great deal of trial and error to find some "safe" foods as well as to find a dose of medication that controls pain.

7 ▶ SLEEP OR LACK THEREOF

The chapter will cover typical sleep patterns seen in infants and toddlers with GERD. There are many hints for getting your baby to sleep so you can get some rest too. The chapter on positioning and home care has specific information on sleep positions and devices such as wedges to elevate the bed for sleeping.

Note: If your baby or child does not have sleep issues, count your blessings and skip this chapter.

Why is Sleep so Difficult?

Let's start with the physical differences in your baby's experience. During the day, your baby is probably upright most of the time. The esophagus is in a vertical or upright position. A baby has a greater chance of keeping food in the stomach and may experience less pain from reflux when upright.

At night, a baby sleeping on a flat surface doesn't have gravity to help keep the food in the stomach since the esophagus is horizontal. There is a better chance that the stomach contents will escape from the stomach and enter the esophagus. We all know what happens from there. The acid irritates the esophagus or causes choking and begins the night waking cycle once again. Now you understand why it is possible to have a relatively happy baby by day and a screaming baby at night.

At the same time that gravity and positioning are allowing more reflux episodes, the LES or lower esophageal sphincter is more relaxed, allowing food and stomach contents to backwash. During sleep, children with reflux also experience a decrease in swallowing and saliva which helps to wash down the reflux during the day.

Just when you thought there could not be any more bad news, added to the mix are other health issues associated with reflux and poor sleep.

Respiratory illness	**Enlarged tonsils**
Teething	**Constipation**
Ear infection	**Sleep apnea**
Food intolerances	**Asthma**

Sleep Patterns...What's Normal?

While we know there is a range of "normal" sleep patterns for infants and children, it is likely that reflux has prevented

---

Jan says:

Even adults say sleep and reflux don't mix! A recent Gallup study indicated that a high percentage of adults with reflux report that poor sleep is the most difficult quality of life issue they face. Adults with GERD report more night-waking, night pain and difficulty getting uninterrupted sleep. The interrupted sleep affects their ability to concentrate and work effectively during the day. No wonder our babies cry out at night!

I often tell parents about the Gallup Study to illustrate how common nighttime GERD and sleep issues are for babies to adults with GERD. Reflux is a 24 hour disease and sleep problems affect everyone, regardless of your age. The only difference is adults can fill out surveys to express themselves and babies end up crying to tell the story.

---

any type of normal sleep pattern or routine in your household. Since you have already read all of the baby books, I will spare you all of the details about what is "average" and "normal." Perhaps you will recognize your baby among the typical sleep patterns below.

Poor sleeper 24/7: This baby naps poorly by day and is a restless sleeper by night. She seems to sleep less than other babies of similar age and weight. She may take

---

A GERD Dad Says...

He was so exhausted from being awake all day that he somehow managed to stay asleep all night.

---

short cat naps during the day or not sleep at all. She may only sleep on your shoulder or in a sling or carrier. She doesn't sleep more than a few hours at night without waking up. But, then again… she may sleep for a long stretch of the night!

Arms (yours) sleeper: She falls asleep easily in your arms but wakes up the moment you place her in her crib.

Awakens in pain: You recognize the scenario: she wakes up without warning from a peaceful sleep and cries out suddenly, as if she is in intense pain. You try, but it is often difficult to console her no matter what you try.

Noise maker: There may be an increase in coughing, grunting, gulping, throat clearing and noisy breathing as your baby struggles to clear her airway and esophagus at night. Your baby may sleep through these episodes or wake up, depending on her sleep cycle.

Light sleeper: The light sleeper awakens with the least sound or for no apparent reason. You tiptoe around the house while she is napping and lunge for the phone on the first ring.

All night eater: This baby wakes up frequently and seems to want to eat, even after the newborn period and when weight is within a normal range.

Perpetual motion: Some infants and children are in constant motion all night. She might twist and turn, throw herself about and bang her arms and legs in an attempt to find a comfortable position and sleep through the discomfort. Medical treatment can often decrease the amount of pain and may make your baby's sleep more restful.

Tips for Getting a Baby with Reflux to Sleep at Night

Managing the pain: When a baby wakes at night it is because pain keeps her from sleeping. Medical treatment needs to manage symptoms if your baby is to get the rest she needs.

Check out "Positioning" in GER: The chapter on positioning provides many options for finding a comfortable sleep position and elevating the bed if the doctor has recommended it.

When You've Tried Everything...

I tried everything and found that co sleeping in a bed was the best way to get the most sleep possible. I will be honest, I co-slept with my daughter until she was 3 years old and still do sometimes. I refused to let her cry it out as long as I knew she suffered from reflux. Let me tell you she is the best at going to sleep now at three years old.

◆

When we put the baby in our bed, none of us got any sleep. We compromised by putting a large mattress on the floor in his room and one of us would sleep with him when he needed it.

Co-sleeping: In many cultures, it is accepted practice for an infant or toddler to sleep with her parents. In this country, it is expected that babies will sleep in their own crib in a separate room. Some parents believe that sharing the bed makes it easier to nurse and care for a baby who wakes up frequently. Parents also report that they feel closer to their baby and more in touch with her needs.

Easy on the night feeding: A common treatment for reflux is to go to bed on an empty stomach. Your doctor may recommend decreasing or eliminating night feeding after 6 months unless weight gain is an issue and 24 hour a day feedings are medically necessary. If your baby absolutely needs a drink at night, see if you can wean her to water only.

Keep the focus on sleep: Your baby's sleep environment needs to be strictly sleep oriented. Make it clear that night is for sleeping, not playing. The room should remain dark and quiet. If the sheet is covered with vomit, place a thick towel over it rather than changing the whole bed. Make sure she is wearing super absorbent diapers and comfortable pajamas to ensure she isn't waking from being cold or wet.

Calming baby by the book: There are several excellent books that teach parents simple but effective techniques to

Jan Says:

During the year she did not sleep through the night, I thought that I was losing my mind. I am usually very organized and I found myself misplacing the phone bill or driving the wrong way to the food store. When I talked to people, I couldn't remember words or names. It was very demoralizing. People make jokes about "new mother haze" but I had it for much longer!

I am happy to report that it is a survivable condition and she did eventually learn to sleep all night. Surprisingly, most of my brain power has returned too!!

calm their baby and help them to sleep. It is likely that there will be some excellent ideas for a refluxer too. Try not to blame yourself or the book if the advice isn't totally effective for you. Remember, your baby has a medical condition that may make calming and comforting extra challenging.

8 ▶ FEEDING: FROM BABY WRESTLING TO CONTENTMENT

A special diet and feeding methods/techniques are more often than not a vital part of the GERD treatment package. Your baby will most likely experience the typical feeding pattern of fussing during or after eating. However, some babies will exhibit more worrisome feeding patterns. This chapter will describe the feeding patterns seen in infants and toddlers with reflux and offer the feeding methods and techniques doctors, therapists and parents have found to be useful to reduce GERD symptoms. While there are a variety of feeding methods and techniques to reduce symptoms, you and the doctor will need to develop a feeding plan that addresses the needs of your infant or toddler.

Parents often describe eating, sleeping and crying as the biggest challenges they face when caring for an infant or toddler with GERD. Sometimes, the feeding challenges top the list of worry and frustration. If you can't nourish your baby because she doesn't want to eat or it keeps coming up, it may seem to be a reflection of your parenting. Remember that it mostly likely is not!

It is important to manage your stress and find support to decrease isolation during this difficult period. Your baby can feel your stress and anxiety about feeding and may react by crying or fussing even more.

Typical Feeding Patterns with GERD

Most babies and toddlers with GERD experience a feeding pattern that reflects a reaction to the pain and discomfort of reflux. The pain of hunger gets replaced with the pain of reflux at each feeding.

Fussing and Crying During or After Feeding

Does your baby fuss, cry and pull away from the breast or bottle? Does it feel like you are wrestling your baby and trying to find a comfortable position for both of you? Some babies begin nursing or drinking eagerly, then they pull away and fuss/protest for the rest of the feeding.

Babies who cry and fuss during feeding are probably experiencing pain with eating. Her tummy wants food but her throat and esophagus can't handle the pain. No wonder she acts confused and agitated during a meal. On the other hand,

---

GERD Moms' Experiences...

My daughter would aggressively attack the bottle for a few seconds, and then suddenly stop with a cry. This pattern escalated until she didn't really want the bottle, only taking it once the hunger pain was worse than the reflux pain.

---

your baby may finish her meal without a whimper. A full stomach may cause bloating, however, and cries of pain may follow each meal.

Other babies do not experience pain until long after a meal has occurred. As the food is digested, it is mixing with acid. Wet burps or spit ups that occur after the meal become more acidic and may hurt more.

It may seem like she is unhappy whether or not her stomach is full or empty. In fact, some parents report that their fussy babies do not signal the need to eat. Even if they skipped a feeding, it would not make a great deal of difference in comfort.

Overeating

Your baby may want to eat constantly to soothe her throat or for comfort and end up over eating. Overeating may cause bloating and fullness. If she starts crying shortly after eating, it might be tempting to offer her more food. See if distraction, a pacifier or burping ease her discomfort.

COMFORT EATER

The comfort eater wants to eat and drink 24/7. She may want to nurse constantly whether awake or asleep to soothe the burning in her throat. She may want to eat frequent small meals so her stomach doesn't get too full, causing bloating and pain. Often, comfort eaters grow rapidly and may even be overweight. Older children who are comfort eaters may graze all day, seldom eating a real meal.

Worrisome Feeding Complications

Sometimes you'll find that your baby's feeding patterns are so far outside what is normal that you begin to worry. Trust your instincts! Add this behavior to your list for the next doctor's visit, or head to the emergency room if it seems appropriate.

SLEEP FEEDING

Sleep feeding, sometimes referred to as dream feeding, occurs when an infant is experiencing a great deal of pain from eating. She can turn off the pain by eating while asleep. You may find that you wait for your baby to go to sleep to initiate feeding. Other times, your baby protests and cries during a meal and falls into an exhausted sleep. Then you can begin the feeding. Sleep feeding works well with young infants because they are likely to sleep for long hours. Toddlers may need to be fed all night after a day of feeding refusal.

Parents find themselves waiting for their sleep feeders to go to sleep so they can feed them and get their child the calories she needs. Of course, the goal of treatment is to manage the reflux. Sleep feeding may offer a short term feeding solution as you work toward decreasing pain, but it is important to remember it is an interim tactic not the best solution.

A Feeding Therapist Says...

I am very concerned about the baby that dream feeds; to me it is a red flag, telling me that the baby is very stressed about feeding. It is developmentally necessary for a baby to process hunger and satiety. Dream feeding takes this process away.

Joan Comrie. MS. CC-SLP

FEEDING STRIKE

A baby who experiences pain with each feeding may decide that she is going to "fix" the problem all by herself—she

---

Feeding Jack

Feeding Jack was the hardest thing I ever did. I tried every bottle, nipple and formula I could find. I swaddled him, rocked him and held him but nothing worked. Then, at four months, he stopped taking the bottle altogether. Feeding was just too uncomfortable for him.

---

is simply going to stop eating. A *feeding strike* means that your baby is refusing nourishment by mouth. A *feeding aversion* is similar to a feeding strike: when a baby associates feeding with pain, just the sight of the bottle or breast is enough to cause distress.

You may want to keep track of the amount she drinks and the number of wet diapers and report this information to the doctor. It may be necessary to go to the emergency room if the doctor is not available.

Babies dehydrate very quickly, so it is important to have your baby evaluated by a doctor if you suspect she has significantly reduced the amount she is eating. The doctor will evaluate your baby to consider if an illness such as an ear

> ### *When the doctor saw her...*
>
> Our doctor wanted to see what happened when I fed her. Just as soon as I showed my baby the bottle, it was as if someone had pinched her. Our doctor said she didn't believe it until she saw it with her own eyes.

infection is causing loss of appetite or if pain from reflux is causing a feeding strike.

> ### *A GERD Mom's Experience...*
>
> She just clamped her little mouth shut and refused to take my breast all day. My mom tried giving her a bottle of formula and we even tried oral hydration drink. We were desperate. My mom held her while I worked to get a few drops of expressed breast milk into her mouth with a medicine dropper. It took an hour to get one ounce in. I finally called the pediatrician and he said to bring her right in. After being examined by the doctor, she was admitted to the hospital for dehydration.

FAILURE TO THRIVE

The term *failure to thrive* used to imply that a child was neglected or abused, missing developmental milestones as well as not growing as expected. Today, this loaded term has lost its original meaning and is now commonly used to mean poor weight gain.

In some cases, a baby with reflux will eat so little or vomit such large quantities that growth is compromised. In older children, picky eating and restricted diets may lead to poor nutrition and growth. Failure to thrive is a medical condition that needs to be monitored closely by the physician. You may need to bring your baby to the doctor for frequent check ups and weight checks. In rare cases, a baby may need to be hospitalized for severe failure to thrive.

Having a baby who is either underweight or a poor eater can be very difficult emotionally. Having a baby who is both can be very traumatic. It is hard to remember that you are a good mother when you can't even feed your own baby enough to keep her from starving. It can be hard to keep your perspective in the face of this.

Growth charts are a standard way of monitoring growth but they need to be balanced with common sense. If the baby's parents are very small and the baby starts small, there is no reason to expect she should be in the middle of the chart. The doctor will watch weight, length and head circumference for trends on the chart that indicate a worrisome pattern. There are several special growth charts including one for premature

---

A GERD Mom's Experience...

My son started throwing up at 10 days old. He was never hungry. It took him two hours to finish 2 ounces of formula. Needless to say, he grew very slowly.

When my pediatrician uttered the words...

"Failure to Thrive" I was reduced to tears. I was scared. I was angry. I was doing more than was humanly possible for my daughter, yet she wasn't thriving!?! I was hurt. It kind of struck at what it is to be a mother, I wasn't a good nurturer. I thought the "diagnosis" was heartless and almost changed pediatricians. For awhile it really affected my ability to work with him to help my daughter.

---

babies and even one for Asian babies who tend to be a bit small.

Infant Feeding Treatments

Be sure to review Part 1, "GER." The important and detailed feeding information included there is appropriate, whether your baby has GER or GERD. Recommendations found there include:

Breastfeeding: Breast milk is considered to be a beneficial diet for many babies with GERD since it is easy to digest.

Special Formula: Some babies benefit from a special formula, especially if there is evidence of Milk Soy Protein Intolerance (MSPI) in addition to GERD symptoms.

Thickening Feeds: Thickening breast milk or formula may reduce vomiting.

Small, frequent feedings: Feeding a smaller amount of breast milk or formula at each meal puts less pressure on the stomach. As you reduce the amount provided at each feeding, it will be necessary to increase the number of total feedings per day.

Positioning: The doctor may recommend holding the baby upright after a meal to reduce vomiting.

Burping: Frequent burping during and after a feeding may reduce pain and discomfort from the pressure of a full stomach.

TRANSITIONING FROM INFANT FORMULA

You may be wondering when you can stop using that expensive infant formula and begin giving your toddler a milk-based diet. Your first step would be to consult with the doctor on signs that would indicate your baby is ready. Some toddlers need to stay on infant formula past a year. Often, a toddler can begin using a toddler formula or a nutritional drink for children ages 1-12 years. A few brands of nutritional drinks are available in the formula aisle. Your doctor can recommend more specialized toddler formula for a special diet.

Some toddlers are not ready to try a new drink and show a strong preference for the bottle and infant formula. Some parents have success with gradually mixing the infant formula with the toddler beverage. To prepare an eight ounce bottle, mix one ounce of the new beverage with seven ounces of infant formula. Every few days add a few more ounces of the toddler beverage until you have made the transition.

The doctor and dentist will strongly urge you to get rid of the baby bottle after age one. However, you may need to be flexible about transitioning to a cup. If you change from an infant formula and use a cup all at once, it is likely there will be some protesting. Infant feeding issues may lead to some caution about trying new textures or flavors. She may be a little concerned about the spoon and bib after just starting to feel "safe" about drinking from a bottle.

DELAY THE INTRODUCTION OF SOLID FOODS

If your baby is happily eating baby food from a jar and grabbing your bagel while she sits on your lap, there is no need

---

Feeding Doesn't Feel Good...

My oldest son (without reflux) ate from a spoon at exactly 4 months of age. He would cry if I didn't shovel it in fast enough! My second son had severe reflux and we were lucky to get him to take a bottle, much less baby food from a spoon. Feeding was not pleasurable to him, and he needed to stay with bottle feeding a lot longer. There was no way I was going to play around with his feeding and add something new. We were both recovering from the work of feeding him while he was in pain. I had to introduce foods a lot more slowly, and it took him a long time to think that food was "safe" let alone "fun."

---

to read this section. However, if your baby doesn't seem thrilled with sitting in a high chair and eating from a spoon or she cries during a meal, read on.

It may be necessary to delay the introduction of solid foods such as baby food from a jar or mashed table foods. Feeding skill development may be delayed if there has been an interruption in feeding due to food refusal or a feeding tube. Just as you needed to move at a slower pace with the bottle, you may need to delay the introduction of baby food, too.

It is hard to say when your little one should start eating solids. Many pediatricians recommend beginning solid foods between 4-6 months. You may find that your baby is ready to eat and eager to try new tastes and flavors. If your baby is clamping her mouth shut or looks uncomfortable during or after a meal, she may be telling you that she is not ready. Some of the baby foods may be high in acid (peaches, apples) causing a burning sensation on an irritated esophagus. If your baby has a swallowing problem (*dysphagia*), the food will cause choking and coughing.

GERD AND PICKY EATING

While medical treatment may have healed the esophagus and decreased the pain, some toddlers continue to experience some level of distress about eating. Your toddler may learn to eat at a slower pace than other children. This can include delayed feeding milestones such as using a spoon or cup as well as eating skills (from pureed to chunky or crunchy table food). In any case, eating isn't necessarily the easiest part of the day for you or your toddler.

It seems to take forever!

It seemed like she was a picky eater forever...chicken, potatoes and rice. Over and over...but over time she started to try a lick here, a lick there. Now she eats just like any other child.

You may feel that all your care and caution has caused your child to become a picky eater. Perhaps you have developed "waitress syndrome" out of desperation to get your child to eat anything. Maybe you bought pretty plates and fancy straws to encourage your child to have a good attitude about eating.

Think of it this way: your picky eater will most likely eat you out of house and home by adolescence – as long as you don't push her too hard before her stomach is ready. The bottom line is your child has a medical condition that makes feeding difficult for *anyone*. It is best to introduce new foods and feeding methods slowly and allow your toddler to develop a positive attitude about eating.

VITAMINS AND MINERALS

Infants and children who are not eating from all food groups and growing slowly may benefit from vitamin and mineral supplements. Ask the doctor before you turn to supplements. If you and your doctor agree that vitamins and

86

mineral supplements are appropriate, keep in mind that vitamins can be harsh on sensitive stomachs. You may have to try several brands before finding one your child can tolerate.

Be careful about mixing liquid vitamins into drinks and foods. Infants and toddlers with GERD are likely to detect a new flavor and may refuse to eat or reject the food in the future. You don't want to undo the successes from all the hard work you and your baby have done!

Special Situations

Try as hard as you and your baby may, sometimes expert advice can be helpful. Your doctor's and your concerns may suggest turning to solutions that offer important assistance in your efforts to maintain a *healthy* baby with GERD.

DEALING WITH FEEDING ADVICE

Helpful friends and relatives will most likely offer advice on feeding your baby and when to start solids. Some will warn you that there is a critical time to begin to introduce baby food or it will be difficult for your baby to learn to eat. Others will tell you that she needs to be exposed to all textures; flavors and food groups or she will not eat a variety of foods later on.

> ### *It can be so frustrating...*
>
> My mother must have said a hundred times, "When you were a baby, I fed you this way and you were just fine!" I just wanted to scream!
>
> ◆
>
> I always felt like friends and relatives were judging me. We all know spoiling your child is "parenting sin" #1 and giving in to a picky eater is "parenting sin" #2.

You may feel offended by feeding advice from others because it seems like a reflection of your parenting. But the reality is: there are no rules for feeding a baby with reflux and there is no magical "right" way. Trust your instincts and you will find the best way to feed your baby.

CONSULTING A DIETICIAN

Many kids who eat a limited variety of foods or have a small appetite still manage to eat a fairly healthy diet and grow well. If you are trying an elimination diet or feeding a picky toddler, you may want to consult with a dietician. If your baby or toddler only eats from two food groups, you may want to track her intake over several days and show the list to a dietician just to be sure she is getting all the vitamins and nutrients she needs. A dietician with a background in reflux and dealing with picky eaters can offer guidance and strategies. However, many of the standard recommendations for weight gain such as adding high fat foods to boost calories (i.e. butter and half-and-half) may not be appropriate for children with reflux.

SENSORY ISSUES

Some infants and toddlers with reflux develop sensitivity to the touch, taste and smell of food, a condition resulting from their long term feeding problems. When we eat, the sensory system processes sensations created by food, sending a message to the brain; while a particular food may taste fine or feel normal on your tongue, the taste and feel may be awful to someone with a sensory problem.

When we eat, we process all sensory information and the results have a huge impact on our inclinations toward eating. If pain has been associated with feeding, it is possible for the sensory system to under-react or over-react to food. For instance, a child may have a hyperactive gag reflex: every time a textured food touches the back of the mouth, a strong gag reflex is activated. The opposite happens if the sensory system reacts slowly: food may be in all the wrong places and start to go down the wrong tube. Gagging can occur if the sensory system does not signal the brain fast enough to prepare for another bite of food.

A child who avoids mouthing toys and doesn't like new tastes and textures may have an overly active sensory system. A child may appear upset or agitated if someone touches in or around the mouth or even the cheeks and chin. Attempts to put textured food in her mouth will often result in crying, avoidance, choking and vomiting. To avoid stimulating an over-active sensory system, a child may insist on a liquid diet or pureed foods. She may want a very bland diet and become upset if foods other than the "safe" foods are introduced.

Get help early rather than later if you suspect a problem with sensory issues. A speech language pathologist or an occupational therapist with knowledge of feeding problems may be consulted to evaluate the nature of the sensory problem and offer treatment to normalize the sensory processing system.

A WORD ABOUT TUBE FEEDING

You may have heard about tube feeding as a possible feeding method for an infant who is growing poorly or who has complications when eating by mouth. While tube feeding does increase intake, it can also overfill the stomach and increase reflux and vomiting. That is why tube feeding may be a last resort method of providing nourishment.

> ### *A GERD Mom Says...*
>
> I had done everything I could to feed my daughter and I was exhausted from the effort.
> Although, it was a hard decision, I finally agreed to tube feeding. The tube helped her grow and have the strength to start feeding therapy.

If you and the doctor agree to use tube feeding, it will be one of two kinds:

A Nasogastric (NG) tube is a thin flexible tube that is inserted into the nose and down into the stomach. A syringe may be attached to the tube and liquid nutrition such as breast milk or formula is poured into the tube and directly into the stomach, bypassing the mouth. Because the tube can be irritating to your baby it is often used as a short term feeding intervention during an acute illness or feeding problem.

A Gastrostomy (G) tube may be recommended if it is determined that tube feeding is needed for a longer period of time. This tube is inserted through a small incision in the abdomen into the stomach and is used for long-term intervention.

A Feeding Story

I've been through feeding hell with my daughter...and made it to the other side. She had flared up horribly when we introduced solids at 6 months and it took forever to get the fire out. We went on medication and finally the screaming stopped. But she wouldn't eat; she wouldn't go near the kitchen where I had the high chair. She'd scream bloody murder. She got her nutrition nursing every hour on the hour at night while she slept. I finally called the pediatric gastroenterologist and his nurse gave me memorable advice: relax and enjoy your baby. I hung up in disgust.

But, she got me thinking about what I was doing to my daughter. I was so desperate for her to eat that I always had a baggie full of Cheerios in my pocket. We'd be out on a walk and I would be stuff them into her mouth rather then let her to enjoy herself; I'd distract her with videos and stuff food into her face.

I took the nurse's advice and willed myself to relax and enjoy my baby. This was the most difficult thing I have ever done. I decided to try letting her be in control of her eating. If she wanted to eat, fine. If not, well she could nurse eight times at night. I took all the pressure off of her.

A couple of weeks later she wanted to come into the kitchen, but not into the high chair; then the high chair, but not eating. Finally, she nibbled. She gained confidence that eating was no longer painful...and that I wouldn't be "encouraging" her to eat. For the past year she eats with such gusto and enjoyment! She loves to eat! She tries EVERYTHING—not one hint of picky eater with her.

I know none of this would have worked if her reflux wasn't under super control. That's the cornerstone. Even when the pain behavior stops, it can take weeks for the esophagus to heal. But, what was wrong was I couldn't hear until I let go of my anxiety. Really listening to my baby—letting *her tell me* when she was ready–worked for us.

9 ▶ THE REFLUX ROLLER COASTER: DIAGNOSIS TO TREATMENT

Some diseases have a very clear path from diagnosis to treatment. A blood test or x-ray confirms the disease or rules it out. If the test is positive, the doctor and patient can begin treatment with confidence.

Unfortunately, such clarity is rare for families whose child has GERD (Pediatric Gastroesophageal Reflux Disease). The road to a GERD diagnosis is paved with many false starts and alternative routes. There are tests used to diagnose and treat GERD, but a test may not be necessary or it may not yield the information needed to guide treatment. For the majority of babies with GERD symptoms, diagnosis and treatment can involve no testing at all. So get ready for a process of diagnosis that will be frustrating, seem endless....and all this the while your baby is in pain.

Jan says:

I used to be so relieved when the doctor said one of my kids had strep throat. It was all so simple and clear from start to finish. First you go to the doctor for one quick visit, swab the throat and get a diagnosis in a matter of minutes. The diagnosis phase was done. The treatment was even easier. After a few doses of "pink medicine" (oral antibiotic), the patient was 100% better.

I used to leave the doctors office thinking, why can't getting a GERD diagnosis and treatment plan be this easy?!

Getting a Diagnosis Takes Time... Except When It Doesn't

A recent study confirmed what many parents of babies and children with GERD already know: it can take weeks or months and many doctors' appointments to get a diagnosis of GERD. In the early stages, GERD may look like GER, a far more common reflux condition. Part 1 of this book is devoted to GER (Gastroesophageal Reflux). You will find many of the issues and illnesses referred to here, elaborated and discussed there.

With GERD, it may take parents and doctors some time to see a pattern of symptoms, rule out other conditions and identify complications. Part of the problem is that we don't have a "one size fits all" to aid in the diagnosis of GERD: one baby has weight loss while another is on the top of the growth chart; one baby cries constantly while another cries only at night. Symptoms differ from baby to baby, and the path to diagnosis is equally diverse.

> ### *Matthew's Story*
>
> Little Matthew seemed to get every cold and illness that his brother brought home from preschool. The doctor said it would get better as his immune system matured. But he was always on the bottom of the growth chart and seemed pale and sickly. It took almost two years before he was diagnosed with GERD.

> ### *A Parents' Experience...*
>
> He started choking when I burped him. All of a sudden, he turned blue and went limp. I screamed for my husband to call 911 and he was rushed to the hospital. After a blur of worry and confusion and a whirlwind tour of the hospital from the blood lab to radiology, he was discharged with a diagnosis of GERD.

The diagnosis process starts with you, the parents. As your child's primary care giver and advocate, you may have a gut feeling that something is wrong and will bring those concerns to the doctor. At first, because there is significant overlap of GER and GERD symptoms, your baby's doctor may want to watch and observe the baby over time for symptoms to gradually change or worsen.

This slow and steady diagnostic path is most likely what your child's reflux will follow. However, it is possible you and your baby will be one of the fortunate few where your baby has clear symptoms of GERD and a diagnosis can be made far more quickly. This is where your observation and documentation of your baby's symptoms proves its value. After the pediatrician has examined your baby, she will ask you some questions about her feeding, sleep and behavior at home. If you have the answers in hand and the information you give shows a clear pattern of classic symptoms, the doctor's knowledge and experience with GERD can sometimes confirm a diagnosis within a limited period of "wait and see".

A GERD Mom Says...

She had a bad case of colic when she was an infant but it went away when she was a few months old. I noticed that she was a very picky eater and barely ate any food at all. She mostly drank from her bottle; even at age two she gagged at the sight of food. The pediatrician referred her to a feeding clinic. She was diagnosed with GERD and a swallowing disorder. It took months of feeding therapy to get her off the bottle and eating with a spoon.

A far more frightening route to a quick diagnosis is when a baby or toddler experiences a sudden, serious medical emergency such as apnea or ALTE (Apparent Life Threatening Event). Because a possible underlying cause of this condition is reflux, your baby will be evaluated right away. Often a baby will be brought to the emergency room or admitted to the hospital. A specialist may examine the baby and tests performed, giving the doctor a quick summary of the problem. A diagnosis may be made then and there under these circumstances.

DIAGNOSIS: A TRIAL OF TREATMENT

The first and simplest way to confirm that your baby has GERD is to start treating her as if she has GER and see if it helps. You may be told to try several home care treatments for a week or so and report back on whether they help. The doctor may also give your baby an anti-reflux medication to see if that makes a difference. Trying a treatment to confirm a diagnosis is called *Empiric Treatment*. The Latin and Greek roots of the word empiric are related to the terms try, experience, knowledge and skill.

This may seem really odd to you and it might make you wonder whether the doctor really knows much about reflux. However, the Guidelines for the Evaluation and Treatment of Gastroesophageal Reflux in Infants and Children, written by the North American Society of Pediatric Gastroenterology, Hepatology and Nutrition (NASPGHAN), do not recommend testing for babies with typical reflux unless they have unusual symptoms or "warning signs" of other diseases, significant complications of reflux, or they don't respond to treatment. When it comes to reflux, empiric treatment is a practical and acceptable approach.

The Doctor Said My Baby Needs a Test

Testing is part of the diagnosis and treatment of GERD. However, many infants and children are diagnosed with GERD without ever needing a test. Your diagnostic journey may or may not include testing. While this book does have a chapter full of detailed descriptions of the common tests used to diagnose GERD, go to it when testing is suggested by your doctor. It may be tempting to read about the tests and suggest to the doctor that a particular test is needed. If your child has already been diagnosed with reflux and you end up persuading the doctor to perform the test, don't be disappointed if the test report states: "the patient has reflux!"

News that your baby needs a test may stir up a great deal of anxiety and stress. No one likes to subject her baby or child to medical procedures, sedation and X-rays. It is important to understand fully what will happen during the test and what information the test will yield. By asking questions and letting the doctor know your concerns, you can work together to make the best decision for your child and you will feel more confident about doing the test. If you're confident, your child will respond much more positively to the experience.

THE ROLE OF TESTING

During the period of time when you and the doctor are watching and observing symptoms, a test may be indicated to rule out other illnesses or problems. It is also an option if your baby has worrisome symptoms or does not respond to treatment. Testing is also a way to monitor progress, guide treatment or identify other medical issues that affect success in the treatment GERD.

For instance, a baby with projectile vomiting may need a test to rule out an intestinal blockage or malrotation. Likewise, a blood test or stool sample may be used to assess the overall health of the baby and rule out other medical reasons for the symptoms.

It you spend some time at an on-line discussion forum, you will likely hear a lot of discussion about testing and test results. Remember, for each child the symptoms of reflux will differ, requiring a different approach to diagnosis and testing; your doctor is in the best position to decide the appropriate approach to treatment and/or diagnosis.

As your baby's advocate, your job is to ask questions and learn. If the doctor determines that a test is needed, go to the specific test description in this book for detailed information on everything from how to prepare your little one to what will happen during and after the test. It offers you a quick introduction that will begin your education.

QUESTIONS TO ASK THE DOCTOR

It is important to ask the doctor several key questions:

What is the goal of testing-what are you trying to learn?
How is the test performed?
Can you treat her without doing a test?
What are the risks involved (sedation, exposure to X-rays, discomfort, IV, infection).

You might also ask:

Can I be there during the test?
Will it be painful or uncomfortable? How can we remedy this?
Where will the test be done (office, hospital)?
Is there another test that will answer our questions better?

PREPARING FOR THE TEST

The doctor's office will provide specific information such as location of the test and arrival time, along with fasting and medication instructions. Make sure you understand the doctor's orders and ask questions before the day of the test. There may be different restrictions depending on the age of your baby or child and her typical diet.

You will need to know:

What time should we arrive?
Are there eating restrictions before the test?
Should she have her medication the day of the test?
What should I bring?

You might also want to ask:

Is she allowed to have a toy or a blanket?
Is there a TV or other bedside entertainment?
Should she wear/not wear certain clothes?

There may be other practicalities to attend to as well. Remember that many insurance plans require pre-authorization and a written referral; find out if yours is one. If the test requires fasting or traveling a distance to a far away location, you might need to make additional arrangements. If you are traveling some distance, it is a good idea to pack a small bag with extra clothes, food and other necessities in case there is a delay or schedule change. It is often helpful to bring a family member or friend to help you on the day of the test and offer moral support. It is unlikely siblings will be allowed in the testing area.

Common Concerns about Medical Procedures

It is very likely you will have questions and concerns about testing depending on your previous experiences and familiarity with hospitals and medical care. Know that your child is watching you, mirroring your beliefs and attitudes. It is important to use good coping strategies and to ask for help if you are anxious about medical procedures. Knowledge and information makes it easier to maintain a calm, open demeanor—even if you're quaking on the inside! Being prepared will make the experience less traumatic for your child...and for you!

A Parent's Experience...

I kept saying, "I don't want to be there for the actual procedure, but I want to be with my toddler until she is asleep and then see her as soon as she wakes up." The staff didn't exactly understand that. When they finally allowed me in the recovery room, I was filled with anxiety and she was howling. Next time, I will be more insistent.

SEPARATION ANXIETY

Sometimes parents are more anxious about being separated from their baby than concerned about the actual test. Be sure to tell the staff your concerns.

A toddler may be most anxious about separation and fear of strangers. It might help to bring some familiar items from home such as a favorite blanket or teddy as well as a cool new toy to offer diversion.

EXPLAINING THE TEST AND PREPARING YOUR CHILD

It is extremely important to tell your child about the test in a way that is developmentally appropriate.

Inform ahead of time. Always tell a child about the test ahead of time, even if it is a few hours or a day before. If you don't tell your child anything until you drive to the door of the hospital, it may lead to distrust and anxiety later on.

Telling older children: An older child may want more of an explanation of the procedure but remember that you don't need to be too graphic. Use words they can understand and explain things from their point of view. In addition, offer reassurance that you will be there as much as possible.

It Can Make a Difference...

I was so grateful for the "Play Lady" as my daughter called her. The Play Lady helped Sarah put a gown on a rag doll, put on a bandage and insert an IV. My daughter clutched that doll during the whole day in the hospital and proudly showed it to her friends in preschool. It made a world of difference in her attitude to talk about the procedure ahead of time.

White coat anxiety: If your baby or toddler has been a frequent flyer with the doctor's office, she may have developed a fear of the whole medical environment. Some toddlers and young children begin to whimper as soon as the car pulls up to the doctor's office and it is all downhill from there.

Play doctor: It might help to give a toddler the opportunity to play with a doctor kit. The local toy store should have a child-sized version of medical tools for a young child. Let her pretend to give you a shot or fix your boo- boo with bandages and kisses.

Consult an expert: Some doctor's offices and hospitals provide special play therapists to help a child get ready for a medical procedure. Ask your doctor about this well ahead of time.

Dealing with pain: If there is going to be some discomfort, ask the doctor if there is a way to lessen pain. For instance, some doctors use EMLA Cream to numb the skin for an intravenous needle (IV) or provide medication to relax her so she can cooperate.

Alert! Low pain threshold: It is very helpful to alert the doctor ahead of time if you know your child has a very low pain threshold or extreme anxiety about medical procedures. The doctor may be able to prescribe medication or even a special lollipop that has relaxing medication before the tests.

Treatment begins

While there is no "cure" or magic pill for Pediatric GERD, there are many proven and effective treatments of the symptoms. Most infants and toddlers respond readily to treatment and show improvement right away. Again, document, document, document!

> ## *Jan says*
>
> When I talk with pediatricians, they complain that patients' parents are demanding medication for reflux, whether or not the doctor believes it is needed. Yet when I talk with parents, they complain that the doctors' treatment plan doesn't address the symptoms they see at home. I believe both parents and doctors need to communicate clearly. Parents need to respect the wealth of information and training of the doctor…and doctors need to listen carefully to the concerns of parents.

A doctor may gradually add treatments such as diet, positioning and medication in an attempt to find a treatment plan that controls symptoms. It is best to try one new treatment at a time and evaluate the success of each change.

Finding the best treatment plan can take a bit of trial and error. It may seem as if the doctor is randomly writing another prescription or handing over a formula sample. In reality, the doctor is going through a systematic process of evaluating the symptoms and adding one treatment at a time until the symptoms are under control. Most treatments for reflux do not have dramatic results. It is more common for the symptoms to get better gradually over a period of days or weeks.

Your doctor may suggest your baby's treatment start with strong medication or tests and gradually back down the treatment once there is control of the symptoms. Unfortunately, the doctors do not have a test to guide them in predicting which child needs the full strength, aggressive treatment and which child needs the home care/wait and see option. From the parents' point of view, this may seem like a lot of effort and a lot of dead-end treatments.

Most babies respond to a combination of treatments and gradually begin to feel better. Your observations and careful follow through of the treatment plan will go a long way toward helping the doctor make good decisions about any changes or adjustments that may be needed. Make one change at a time so you and the doctor can determine what the best treatment is and to avoid unnecessary alternatives or medication.

Not Sure About Medical Treatment

If your child is diagnosed with GERD, you may find yourself wanting to put off medical treatment at first but then change your mind later. You may feel it is best to tough it out and wait for your baby to outgrow reflux; you can use home care techniques without medicine. While there is a great deal of evidence that your baby will outgrow reflux in a year or two, there is no guarantee when the pain will end and the vomiting will stop. Who knows if your baby is on the six month plan or the three year plan? Could you really continue to clean up vomit and wake up six times a night a year from now? Is it fair to leave your baby in pain that long? You and your doctor might have this conversation several times before making a treatment decision.

Adjusting the Treatment Plan

As your baby begins to feel better, you may wonder if the treatment is still necessary. If you are using an expensive formula or medication, you may wish there were an alternate that was less costly. If your baby is on a strong

---

A GERD Mom Says...

We had tried all the medicines and increased the dose several times. I was completely appalled when the doctor said we needed to get him off all medicines for a week and see what was really going on. I was scared to death to do this and shocked when it worked. The crying stopped. The best we can figure, he must have been having side effects from the medication - like a headache.

---

medication or on a medication with side effects, you may be motivated to decrease or eliminate the medication if it isn't needed. While it is tempting to make adjustments at home, it

101

is vital to consult the doctor before modifying the treatment plan.

During the course of treatment, the doctor may ask you to stop treatment for a few weeks or a month and observe if symptoms return. This is a way for the doctor to assess the need for treatment without doing a test or procedure. You may find that the best treatment is no treatment!

The most beneficial treatments may change a bit as your baby gets older. Babies benefit from treatments that include being held upright after feeding and keeping the head elevated for sleep and play. Toddlers and children respond best to careful eating: avoiding foods that cause symptoms, chewing carefully and eating small, frequent meals.

If a baby or child exhibits new symptoms, you will need to consult the doctor again for advice and recommendations. Again, you might feel pretty knowledgeable about reflux and be tempted to increase the medication or try an over the counter medication on your own. It is always best to consult with the doctor either by phone or during an office visit before changing the plan.

Remember: Your child's treatment plan is also a vital source of diagnostic information; changing the treatment impacts ongoing diagnosis as your child grows. Work with your doctor. Do not try any positioning, diet, medication or other treatment without first discussing such changes with your baby's doctor.

MANAGING ANGER AND FRUSTRATION

While you and your doctor work together to diagnose and treat GERD, it is likely you will feel overwhelmed by the huge burden of care giving. The addition of extra medical appointments and time consuming treatments can bring additional stress. And all this while you are exhausted! Feelings of anger and frustration consume you. This may be the first time you have ever faced a problem that has no obvious solution. You may feel angry at the disease and the fact that there is no quick fix.

You may find yourself getting angry with your doctor or the medical team. It may seem like they don't understand

A GERD Mom's Experience...

I am so sick of being told that 'babies go through things.' I called my pediatrician this morning to tell her that once again my 10 month old is not eating... how can she think this is normal? We tried a Pediatric Gastroenterologist a couple of months ago. He also looked at me like I was crazy and said, "Don't compare what your baby eats to other babies..." Is it me????

the problem or they are not listening to you. You may feel frustrated about going to the doctor over and over again and find your baby still does not have a clear treatment plan.

Sometimes the office staff or doctors may make comments that are hurtful or seem to imply that you are overusing the medical system by calling so much or getting too emotional.

Yes, I am Frustrated!

The doctor is having me bring her in for a weight check this morning. I know it won't be good, so maybe she'll pay attention then. But I ask why does it have to be like this? I'm an emotional wreck because my days are spent trying to get my baby to eat and no doctor sees a problem with that?

◆

I am a basket case. I feel so hopeless and sad to see my beautiful child suffer endlessly. I want to scream at the doctor, please help me!

Some parents' passion about getting care for their children may appear to be overbearing and annoying to the medical community. It is hard to find balance when you are consumed with fear and worry about your child. You may have been spinning in circles from one specialist to another, tried every treatment and medication on the market and

103

spent long days and difficult nights taking care of a child who just doesn't seem to be getting better. The urgency you feel may not be shared by a physician who is used to treating very sick children; to her, your child may not seem very sick.

It is easy to be labeled as hysterical or over involved if you show a lot of emotion to the doctor about your disappointment and frustration. Rather than leaning on your child's doctor for all the support you need, it may be better to seek out a parent support organization. While many doctors are very supportive to parents, there is nothing like hearing from another parent who has walked in your shoes!

Most important: don't give up. Who wouldn't feel overwhelmed, frustrated and misunderstood? See the chapter on "Homecare" for additional information and coping strategies. Taking care of yourself means you are better able to look out for your baby's interests.

10 ▶ WORKING WITH THE MEDICAL TEAM

Yes, you and your doctor lead Team Reflux but...now we have all these other folks, these "specialists" on our team. When the process of diagnosing and treating your child's gastroesophageal reflux (GER) begins, it is normally with your primary care physician such as a family practitioner or pediatrician. Adding specialists to the Team will likely increase time in doctors' offices, time spent in testing, new information and new advice. Being ready and feeling confident go a long way toward making the experience more positive, and your time well spent.

Who are all of these People?!

Specialists are brought on board at the recommendation of your primary care physician when your child has complications of gastroesophageal reflux disease (GERD) or doesn't respond to treatment. Your child may be treated by one or more of the specialists listed below. How many of these specialists are on your Team Reflux is determined by your child's symptoms and your doctor's reading of those symptoms.

Often, your doctor will refer you to someone. If not, or if you want to seek a second opinion, you need to search for the required specialist directly. Start with the children's hospital or clinic nearest your home; they are good places to find the specialist you need. If at all possible, select a specialist with pediatric training.

Pediatrician: Specializes in the care of children from birth to adolescence.

Pediatric Gastroenterologist: A pediatrician with additional training in diseases of the gastrointestinal tract.

Pediatric Pulmonologist: A medical doctor with additional training in lung diseases affecting children such as asthma, cystic fibrosis and sleep apnea.

Pediatric Otolaryngologist or Ear, Nose and Throat Doctor (ENT): A specialist with training in diseases of the ears, nose and throat such as otitis media (ear infections), sinus infections and upper airway breathing issues.

Pediatric Allergist: A medical doctor with specialized training in pediatric allergic diseases such as food and environmental allergies.

Dietician: A practitioner trained to assess the diet and nutrient (vitamins and minerals) needs of your child and suggest ways to ensure health and growth.

Feeding Team: A team of doctors and specialists, such as a pediatric gastroenterologist, speech language pathologist,

---

When the Experts Can Help...

My son is 17 months old and has had reflux since birth. He refused solids. In fact, he would gag and throw up if we gave him anything thicker than baby food fruit. He had a feeding evaluation, and it was determined that he has what is called, "Sensory Integration Disorder." His therapist told me that it is common in children with reflux. It basically means that their body has a hard time accepting things with texture. It also shows up in some kids as not liking things on their feet or hands. My son did not dive into his 1st birthday cake. Instead, he wiped the frosting off of his fingers immediately. He has been going to therapy for 2 months now. It is a slow process, but I keep seeing improvements.

---

occupational therapist, dietician and psychologist who work together to address the complex feeding and related behavioral issues your child may experience.

Being Prepared for the Doctor Visit

The vast majority of infants and children are diagnosed based on a visit to the doctor for a physical exam, a review of symptoms and a trial of medication or other treatment. Your role is vital in this diagnostic and treatment process. Knowing what *you* need to look for, what your doctor needs to know and how to present that information to the doctor is an essential part of your baby's care.

> ...based upon expert opinion, in most infants with vomiting and older children with regurgitation and heartburn, a history and physical examination are sufficient to reliably diagnose GER, recognize complications [GERD], and initiate management.[1]

A history...what is "a history" and what does that have to do with me? Read on!

WATCH AND DOCUMENT

Document, document, document...What you see and what you know is what the doctor relies on when forming a diagnosis and treatment plan. Your baby or young child cannot speak for herself, so you are her advocate as well as her caretaker. Look back in this book, to the section on "GER" and read "Practical Tips for the Doctor's Visit." This gives you a good idea of what you need to do and tips from other moms and dads on what works best.

Create a summary: Often with GERD, you find yourself describing the problem to a variety of doctors and specialists. You may want to take a moment to write a one page summary with the following information:

Diagnosis
Tests
Illnesses
Current medication/doses

---

1 Colin D. R., Mazur, L. J., Liptak, G. S., Baker, R. D., Boyle, J. T., Colletti, R. B., et al. (2001). Guidelines for evaluation and treatment of gastroesophageal reflux in infants and children: Recommendations of the North American Society for Pediatric Gastroenterology and Nutrition. *Journal of Pediatric Gastroenterology and Nutrition,* 32, Supplement 2, pp. S1-S31. Parents and professionals can download a copy from http://www.naspghan.org by searching archived publications.

If possible, include

weight chart
copies of any tests and lab results
duplicate statements

Add it to your notebook. This will save time and increase the information you can give to what will be a grateful doctor!

A GERD Mom says:

Before appointments, I prepare a list of my questions and fax it to the doctor. It makes me get organized and gives the doctor time to review the chart to see if tests are back, etc. Then the doctor can keep the fax in the chart.

You will be glad too. It is always a terrible feeling to leave an appointment and think, "Oh no! I forgot to tell the doctor!"

Document your baby's day: Don't forget your carefully documented description of your baby's two or three days: when and how she slept, when and what she ate, how much she ate, how much she vomited, her crying, her moments of peace…all this information and more is needed in GERD diagnosis and treatment. As the doctor has you trying this

---

An email from a parent to Jan:

We saw the pediatric gastroenterologist on Monday and did get a diagnosis of gastroesophageal reflux disease. I followed your advice and very carefully charted his day for three days, which greatly helped. I also spent hours preparing a one page sheet of my top three concerns and all the symptoms that went with the concerns. If I hadn't contacted you, I am fairly certain I would have collapsed into a frustrated crying heap in his office; but instead, I was calm because I felt prepared. As a result, the doctor has doubled the amount of medicine that he takes and we start another medicine in three weeks if needed.

---

position or that food, another feeding routine or medication, your documentation is what will inform you both on whether it's working or if another option needs to be tried.

Doing this will not only help you to describe your child's behavior accurately, it will increase your confidence and help calm your anxiety. A calm mom is an effective mom, especially when it comes to GERD.

Medical Records: If your child has complex medical needs, or even if she doesn't, ask for your own copy of all medical tests and reports. Store them in a folder or binder. Bringing this information to each appointment with a specialist is a good idea. Doing this will save the doctor (and you!) from having to request copies of records. Requesting records often means you have to wait for them to be sent to the doctor, only to find out at your appointment that they didn't arrive or didn't make their way into your baby's file.

ADVOCACY AND COORDINATING CARE

Advocacy: You go to the doctor and she listens but doesn't *hear you*...so you politely and firmly hold your ground until she does hear you. Sound like you? Then you already know what it is to be an advocate. It's not complicated: you are someone with a vested interest in the well being of another person who makes decisions on their behalf. Often parents and grandparents act as advocates when seeking medical treatment for a child with GERD. A friend

> ### Jan says:
> Only you know your baby. You are your baby's best advocate. Your baby can't tell what's wrong, and so you have to be his voice. Be persistent and diplomatic. Make them listen to you.

or family member may also serve as an advocate. As an advocate, you need to be respectful and courteous when talking to the doctor and office staff while at the same time standing your ground when you feel that further treatment is warranted.

Coordinating Care: Taking care of your baby may leave you feeling like a nurse. Every morning you make your coffee and line up the syringes of medication; write down the number of episodes of vomiting through the night in your journal; and then make a fresh batch of hypoallergenic formula mixed with cereal or Karo Syrup.

And that's just your morning! After you have gotten everyone fed, cleaned and medicated, there is still more to do. If your child has GERD and other medical concerns, you may be especially busy coordinating medical care. It is time to get on the phone and make medical appointments, call the insurance company to review a claim and of course call the pharmacy about the prescription refills.

Try to find someone to help you with the small details. Over time, you will find the short cuts such as using the automated system or the internet for prescriptions and appointments. Some insurance companies will assign a case manager to help the family navigate the medical care system. The case manager knows how the insurance plan works and can often speed up the process of medical authorization and approval for special situations such as obtaining a prescription formula or getting a medication that isn't on the insurance company's preferred list.

REALITIES OF MODERN MEDICINE

The world of HMOs, new technology and "time saving" devices may make you cozy with apnea monitors and feeding

> ### A GERD Mom Says...
>
> My doctor reviewed my daughters chart with another doctor in the practice because she has a complex case. If my primary doctor is out of the office, I can usually schedule with the other doctor. It saves me from explaining the whole complex history to an unfamiliar doctor and ensures we get more coordinated care.

pumps. A few years ago, a nurse would have knocked on your door with all of this equipment, knowledge and experience. Now, parents assume the responsibility for providing a high level of medical care to their offspring in the comfort of their home...alone.

That isn't all that has changed in medical care; change continues at a rapid rate. Most frustrating and time consuming is how changes have impacted the doctor-patient relationship. The reality is, you may not see the same practitioner all of the time if you are part of a big practice. Many doctors do not have as much time as they want to see patients and coordinate care so the doctor may seem rushed or respond slowly to your phone message.

If your doctor does not hear from you, he/she probably assumes that your child is better. It is your responsibility to report back to the doctor any concerns or complications about the treatments prescribed by the doctor.

> *A GERD Mom Says...*
>
> I couldn't believe that I had to wait so long to get an appointment with the pediatric gastroenterologist. I called another hospital an hour away and the wait was even longer.

Also, it is important to remember that doctors face limitations from insurance companies and complex rules for authorization of treatment and even being told which medications to prescribe. In some specialties such as pediatric gastroenterology, there is a shortage of specialists in some parts of the country, leading to a lengthy wait for an appointment.

CASE MANAGEMENT

Researchers call caretaking the "unplanned career." Well, added to your new "career" as nurse, advocate and care coordinator, there is one more responsibility: case manager. A medical case manager is someone who looks at all the pieces and integrates them into the care and treatment of the patient: medical history, previous treatments, and medical consultations. Using the information available, a plan of action is developed. Ideally, the primary care physician will be the main doctor helping to coordinate care, especially if other specialists are involved. In some cases, a specialist such as a pediatric gastroenterologist will assume the primary role as case manager.

111

It is likely you are the one with the most information. Don't hesitate to speak up and give information that may guide the doctor. All of the little clues can add up and help the doctor make the best decision.

Some parents partner with the doctor, sharing the case management responsibilities. Discuss the pros and cons of various treatments with the doctor, especially if you have already received your medical education from reading books or the internet! It may feel natural to talk with the doctor and then make a decision.

> ### *Making a Plan*
>
> What makes me feel good about my doctor is we lay out a plan of action. He might say:
>
> 1. Start with ___ medication. If that seems to be working, bring him in for a weigh-in every ___ and adjust medication.
>
> 2. If ___ medication doesn't work, we'll go to ____ medication.
>
> 3. If that doesn't work, we...well, we start again!

TIPS FOR MANAGING MEDICAL COSTS

Oh, and another caretaking role deserves mention: bookkeeper. All the doctors' visits, medications, equipment, special food and other costly items will add up. Being prepared and knowing what you can do to keep these costs from sending the family budget into a tailspin will go a long way toward alleviating stress. Here are some options that might help keep chaos at bay.

A Health Care Spending Account: The IRS allows you to set aside money before taxes to pay for medical expenses. The account may allow reimbursement for a positioning device or special formula that isn't covered by the health insurance.

Medical deductions: See if you qualify for the medical deduction on your tax returns. If you aren't sure what is deductible or if you qualify for medical deductions, contact an accountant or bookkeeper for advice. Every little bit helps!

Insurance: Compare insurance options when you renew your coverage. Perhaps you need a different kind of insurance policy now that you have a child with health issues. The high deductible and sparse prescription coverage may have been just fine before kids. Now you may find that a PPO or HMO offers similar services but with more reasonable co-pays.

Government programs: Each state has a Children's Health Insurance Program or CHIP. Families without insurance or with certain income guidelines may qualify for free or very low cost health insurance with coverage for everything from medical care, prescriptions, hospitalization and even dental care. Check with the local health department in your city or county or contact the state health department for information.

11 ▶ MEDICATIONS FOR REFLUX

Medication is one treatment that may be necessary to control symptoms of Gastroesophageal Reflux Disease (GERD). Just as there is no "one size fits all" treatment for GERD, no one medication nor one dosage is best for all infants and children. If you talk to other GERD parents, you will find a variety of brands, combinations and dosages of medication in use. Keep in mind that each baby or child needs to be evaluated by the doctor, who will select a medication and dosage based on the symptoms and treatment goals. By working with the doctor and following the treatment plan, the best medication and dosage for your child will be determined.

This chapter explores many of the issues parents face when deciding on or carrying out a medication treatment plan, including how to actually get the medication in your baby or child successfully. An overview of the medications used to treat GERD is presented in its own chapter. While not inclusive, it does cover those medications that are widely prescribed today by doctors treating GERD.

Common Questions and Concerns

Most parents have many questions as they begin the process of treating their baby's or child's GERD with medication. Questions are a good thing when it comes to medication. Listen to your doubts; if you need clarification, go straight to the source—your doctor and pharmacist—and get some straight answers.

DOES MY CHILD NEED MEDICATION?

Often, home care is enough to relieve the symptoms of reflux, which is why most doctors start out by trying basic treatments first. If the symptoms persist or cause worrisome side effects such as breathing problems or lack of weight gain, you and the doctor may decide to try a trial of medication.

CAN I USE AN OVER-THE-COUNTER MEDICATION?

The antacid aisle of the pharmacy is brimming with over-the-counter medications for heartburn, stomach pain and other related conditions. It may be tempting to try a medication. After all, you don't need a prescription, so how harmful can the medication be? The truth is, selecting a medication and determining the dose is best left to an experienced physician.

Any treatment begins with diagnosis. When your child's doctor selects medication as treatment, she takes into consideration both over the counter and prescription medications. If you have seen a product on the pharmacy shelf, do not hesitate to ask the doctor or pharmacist if the medication is appropriate for your child.

In many cases, an infant or young child will need a small, carefully measured dose or will need to have a pill or capsule made into a liquid by the pharmacist.

Some medications are made for occasional use only and not for daily use over weeks or months.

WHAT IF I DON'T WANT TO GIVE MY CHILD MEDICATION?

Some parents are uncomfortable with the idea of giving an infant or young child medication, preferring home treatment or a "natural" remedy. Some parents have tried chiropractic, naturopathic and homeopathic techniques.

Be sure to discuss your concerns about medication with your doctor and ask for assistance in finding alternate remedies. The several categories of herbals that may be useful for the treatment of reflux need to be part of your home treatment plan. As you and the doctor work toward diagnosis and effective treatment for your baby's GERD, accuracy of information is critical.

Here are the more common alternatives.

Carminatives soothe the stomach and decrease gas.

Demulcents offer a protective barrier for irritated tissue.

Antispasmodic properties in some herbs are often used for digestion.

Gripe water (made from dill, fennel, or ginger) for colic is the most commonly used herbal remedy for babies.

Probiotics are beneficial bacteria found in the stomach. Some types of probiotics—such as acidophilus, lactobacillus and bifid bacterium—may reduce digestive issues such as colic and diarrhea. Some brands of yogurt contain live bacteria; powder, liquid and pill supplements are also available. There is a trend toward adding bifid bacterium to commercially made baby formula, responding to some evidence of its beneficial properties for babies with digestive problems.

Digestive enzymes break down food for absorption and digestion. The body produces digestive enzymes naturally; they are also found in the foods we eat. If the digestive system isn't producing enzymes in the correct quantities, symptoms similar to reflux can arise. Fresh papaya and papaya supplements are thought to aid digestion; however, there is little scientific evidence to support this.

GERD Mom Says...

I only eat organic food and live a healthy lifestyle. There was no way that I was going to give my child medication at 6 weeks of age. By the time she was 10 weeks, I could see that the side effects of untreated reflux were worse than the side effects of the medication. It was like an on/off switch. After just two doses of reflux medication, she stopped shrieking and only fussed and cried if she was hungry or tired. I asked my doctor about herbal or natural medicines. He asked me not to use them without his knowledge and consent. I was surprised to learn that some herbs are quite dangerous for babies. I guess I tend to think "natural" means "safe."

WHAT IS THE STRONGEST MEDICATION AVAILABLE?

After too many days spent comforting a crying baby, it may be tempting to think that a good, strong medication in a high dose will "fix" the reflux. If only it was that easy! While there are many good medications available, there is no treatment that is considered the best or strongest for every infant or child. Use caution when asking for medication because not all crying is due to reflux and giving strong medicine may only give you more side effects without any benefit.

> ### Jan says:
>
> Often, a frustrated parent will say, "I'm sick and tired of this reflux. Just tell me the strongest medication available so I can tell my doctor to give me a prescription."

MY BABY VOMITED HER MEDICATION. WHAT SHOULD I DO?

Ask the pharmacist or doctor if you should wait until the next dose or give the dose again. It is common for a baby to spit up or vomit when a new medication is introduced. However, if this happens each time you give the medication, the problem should be reported to the doctor right away.

WHY ISN'T THE MEDICATION STOPPING THE VOMITING?

Vomiting *may* decrease when an acid-reducing medication is given; however, reflux medications are not supposed to stop vomiting. Ask the doctor or pharmacist to explain the type of medication your child is taking and what to expect as a result of taking the medication.

HOW DO I KNOW IF MY CHILD STILL NEEDS THE MEDICATION?

It is important to have frequent office visits or phone consultations to evaluate the treatment plan. If your child seems to be feeling better, the doctor may gradually decrease the medication or stop increasing the dose. Sometimes, the doctor will ask you to stop the medication for one to two weeks to see if reflux symptoms return.

SHOULD WE SWITCH BRANDS?

If your child is not responding to her medication, the doctor may switch her from one brand to another. This is not

> ### A GERD Mom's Experience...
>
> The doctor told me that he likes brand A because it works better for most kids. Of course, brand B worked much better for my little one because she never follows any expectations!
> ◆
>
> I must say I was disappointed with the medicine. After switching brands and increasing the dose, there was little change in his sleep or feeding. I guess I expected much more.

uncommon. There are many reasons why the doctor's first choice did not work: her metabolism may be different or a hidden ingredient may not be effective for her.

Keep in mind that not all insurance companies cover all brands of medication. Your doctor or the nurse may have to call your insurance company and get authorization to use a particular brand.

CAN I MIX THE MEDICINE WITH HER FOOD?

Use caution when mixing medication into food or formula. The medication may not work as effectively when it is mixed with certain foods. In addition, an infant may dislike the new flavors or get full before finishing the food/ formula, thus reducing the overall dose given.

HOW CAN I GET MY TODDLER TO TAKE MEDICATION?

Use a special spoon or syringe to administer medications so a toddler does not associate eating with yucky tasting medicine. Try not to give medication in the high chair or use feeding utensils. Praise the child when he/she cooperates. It is best to approach reluctant toddlers in a straight forward, non-emotional tone, avoiding anger or punishments.

See compounding and flavoring, discussed below, for additional ideas.

WHAT IF MY CHILD HAS A FEEDING TUBE?

Check with the doctor before putting any medicine in a feeding tube (gastrostomy or nasogastric tube) and follow instructions carefully. Sometimes the tubing becomes clogged or thick medication sticks to the walls of the tubing. The doctor may have to speak to the manufacturer to get directions.

HOW DO I MANAGE THE HIGH COST OF MEDICINES?

This is a major issue for many parents of a baby or child with GERD. Here are some ways to ease the financial burden:

Call the consumer hotline or access the website of the manufacturer of your child's medication. Many pharmaceutical companies offer rebates or downloadable coupons for prescriptions, even if you have insurance.

Join the manufacturer's consumer club to receive ongoing announcements of new rebates and coupons.

When filling a new prescription, ask for a 2-3 day supply before buying the entire 30 day supply. If the medication is not tolerated, you won't be stuck with expensive medication you cannot use or return.

See if your insurance policy has a mail order prescription service for long term medications you know you will need; some mail order services allow you to get a three month supply for one co-pay.

Ask the doctor about using generics or splitting a pill. She may be able to supply you with samples of the medication you can try before filling the prescription.

Ask the doctor for samples of over the counter medications, such as pain relievers and antacids. Their size is perfect for sending to daycare or for travel. Often the sample will have a coupon inside for future savings.

IS THE MEDICATION SAFE?

The Food and Drug Administration approves a drug for use after the manufacturer submits data to prove that it is effective and safe in adults. The drug is then said to be "indicated" or "approved" for use by adults. An FDA approved medication may be prescribed to a child even if it has not been specifically tested on children. This is called an off label use of the medication.

Only a few reflux medications have been approved for infants and toddlers. Medication manufacturers are increasingly testing their medications and establishing safety and dosing recommendations for infants and children. This is vitally important because infants and children may metabolize medication differently than adults and medication safety is an important issue for parents.

All medications, whether it is a pain reliever purchased at the local pharmacy or a prescription medication, have the potential for unwanted side effects. You and your doctor need to decide if the possible side effects of the medication are more serious than the possible risks of not treating GERD.

Potential unwanted side effects are equally possible with homeopathic or "natural" treatments you might use instead of medication. See Part 4 for specific details on a variety of medications.

HOW DO I REPORT PROBLEMS WITH MEDICATIONS?

If your child has had a significant problem with a medication you should discuss the situation with your child's doctor. Ask the doctor if the reaction was typical or unusual. You or the doctor may want to report the problem to the Food and Drug Administration. Doctors are not required to report problems with medications but affected patients and care givers may file a report. Consumers may report adverse reactions to the Food and Drug Administration by phone at 1-888-463-6332, 800-INFO-FDA or on the web at www.fda.gov/medwatch. You may use the on-line form or download the form and mail it to the FDA. You don't need to send medical reports or medical details. Just describe what you saw and if you had to see a doctor for treatment.

What to Know About Giving Medication

Start first by getting instructions. Ask the doctor and/or your pharmacist to explain how to give your baby or child the medication. Take careful notes and refer back to them often. If you are still uncertain or unsure, do not hesitate to call back and ask for clarification. Safety first!

Some medications need to be mixed and measured with a syringe; others need to be given with food or before a meal. Getting started on a routine can be rather complicated; particularly when more than one medication is needed. The first step is, if you can't read your doctor's handwriting on the prescription, ask for the spelling of the drug and write it on the back of the paper.

GERD Moms Say...

First, I would fill all of the syringes for the day. Then, I made a little line of syringes on the counter: two for the am, two at lunch, one at dinner, and two at bedtime. It really gets easier when you develop your own routine.

◆

I write on the medicine bottle in BOLD print the current dose to be given...especially helps for those nights your eyes are not real wide awake. Also if grandma or a babysitter happens to come over to the house they know exactly how much medication to give them. If we have a dose increase, I cover the old dose with a large sticker and write the new dose in large print.

Most medications for reflux are most effective when they are taken on a precise schedule. Work with your doctor and

Another Memory Aid...

I have a wipe-off board that you can put on your refrigerator. I keep a list of the doses and then check off as the day goes along. I found it to be a major brain saver!! Anything to help in those sleep deprived days!!!

pharmacist to make a daily medication schedule. In our hectic lives, parents often find it difficult to remember to give the medication on time. So we often find creative ways to develop a routine.

ASK YOUR PHARMACIST OR DOCTOR QUESTIONS

Don't be shy, don't feel silly, don't feel dumb...these feelings have no place in the lexicon of parent interactions with their child's doctor. This is especially true when you are giving your child her doctor-prescribed medication. Here is a list to get you started. Add to it or select from it...whatever works for you and your child.

What type of medication is this (for example acid reducer, motility medication, or PPI)?

How long will it take to start seeing progress or effectiveness?

When should I call or make a follow up appointment to check on the success of treatment?

What is the exact dose of the medication?

Can I give medication without regard to food or meal times?

Are there special directions or precautions when this medication in combined with other prescription or over-the-counter medications?

Are there any special instructions concerning how to use this medication?

How long should I continue to give this medication?

What side effects should be reported?

How should I store this medication? Can I save unused portions for future use?

123

What should I do if I forget a dose of the medication?
Should I call to have the dosage adjusted every time my child gains weight?

MEASURING MEDICATION

Ask the pharmacist or nurse to show you how to accurately measure the medication. You may need an oral syringe (different than the type of syringe used for a shot) or measuring spoon made just for medication. It is important to

---

Advice from GERD Moms:

I was using a thick syringe that the pharmacy gave me. It squirted the medicine into his mouth too fast and he would gag. Then he would cry and spit out a lot of his medicine which meant that I never knew how much he was really getting. I asked the nurse at the hospital for a suggestion and she gave me a mini syringe. It worked perfectly!! Now he just drinks down the medicine without any fuss. And I must stress the words "without any fuss."

◆

The doctor taught me to put my finger inside her mouth and hold her cheek open while I used the syringe to put the medicine toward the back of her mouth. There aren't as many taste buds back there and she could not spit the medicine out while my finger was in her cheek.

---

measure accurately. Don't rely on the good old kitchen measuring spoons or family teaspoons; they are not accurate enough for some medications. Finally, what works well to get the medicine down one child may not work for your child.

CHANGING A MEDICATION'S DOSAGE

Do not increase or decrease the prescribed dose, and do not stop giving the medication without consulting with the doctor. If your child is not responding to a medication, it is best to call the doctor or pharmacist for advice. Be ready with a clear statement of the effect of the medication on your child or baby.

Remember that side effects may be temporary or may indicate the need to use a different medicine. Sometimes a symptom that first looks like a side effect turns out to be due to something else entirely. When you are considering action, remember that some medicines need to be withdrawn gradually to avoid discomfort or additional symptoms. Your doctor or pharmacist will know this and can advise you accordingly.

ADJUST DOSAGE FOR WEIGHT GAIN

Some medications need to be adjusted for weight. The doctor will use follow up visits to monitor growth and monitor symptoms so she can determine if a change in dosage is needed. One way for the doctor to slowly wean your baby off her medication, is to keep the dose the same as your baby grows.

Your Baby Won't Take Her Medicine

Some babies develop a negative attitude about eating. If your baby is not excited about taking a bottle or a spoon of baby food, it is very likely that taking medication will be just as hard. A combination of pain, regurgitation and fear of having food or medicine in the mouth pretty much guarantees that giving medication will be a struggle. Once again we resort to trial and error to find what "helps the medicine go down" and what doesn't.

While we want our children to have a good attitude about taking medicines, remember to be clear that medicine is not candy. Only adults should give medicine; don't let a sibling or the young child taking the medicine prepare or give the dosage. As always, make sure all medicines are locked up at all times.

From Jan's Blog at www.healthcentral.com:

It can be a real struggle to get your refluxer to take medication. My daughter Rebecca needed all kinds of medication when she was a baby, from reflux medication to antibiotics and vitamins. To say she disliked medicine is putting it mildly. Her little gums would clamp together and she would move her head this way and that to get away from the spoon or syringe. I would insist just as much as she resisted and we would struggle. It looked like some strange form of baby wrestling or child maltreatment. In any case, I was determined to get the medication in no matter how much she protested. She managed to get some of it in before the rest dribbled down her shirt or onto the floor. We both felt pretty worn out from the process. Unfortunately, she needed multiple doses of medication so our little ritual occurred over and over each day. Eventually we worked out a routine and the struggles decreased. Now that I know a great deal more about reflux, I realize she had valid reasons to resist taking medication.

Babies with reflux may struggle with taking medication because:

Fear: Babies with reflux are often afraid of new flavors, colors, textures and temperatures in their mouth. New, unfamiliar foods may cause digestive discomfort so a baby with reflux is inclined to stay with familiar flavors and foods. It is hard for a baby to distinguish between food and medicine so a baby with reflux may decide that anything that goes in the mouth should be approached with extreme caution. Crying, turning away and pursed lips (firmly closing the mouth) are all ways for a baby to express fear and displeasure.

Pain: Many medications will cause pain and irritation from the throat to the stomach when ingested.

Regurgitation: The medication may have tasted bad going down. Imagine how bad it would taste if it was mixed with stomach acid and then came back up again. Rebecca's breath smelled of liquid baby vitamins long after I gave her a dose. I know this had to be unpleasant for her.

Association: A syringe or medication spoon may be associated with a bad taste or an unpleasant experience. We know babies are very smart and it makes sense that they would protest.

Liquid Medicines: Flavoring and Compounding

Does your child make a funny face or turn away when the medicine syringe comes her way? Maybe she knows that the medication has a terrible taste. Try a lick of the medication and see what you think. Now, would you take that?! No medicine works if you can't get it into your child.

Flavoring: Your pharmacist can add special flavoring to the medication to mask even a strong flavor. However, you want to watch out for home flavorings; some, such as chocolate syrup or jelly, can reduce the effectiveness of some medicines, particularly PPIs (Proton Pump Inhibitor). If you think you may want to use home flavorings, check first with your pharmacist when you order the prescription.

> ### *A GERD Mom Says...*
>
> I found a pharmacy that has tons of flavors. They were able to flavor one medication strawberry and the other grape. My daughter loved the flavors and took the medication so easily! The pharmacist also gave me a special oral syringe top for the bottles so it makes it really easy to dose the medication.

Compounding: Many reflux medicines only come in adult dosages (pill or capsule) and a pharmacist must make a form that an infant or child can take. Pills are often made into a liquid "compound" with added sweeteners and anti-bittering flavorings. Also, some medicines are already available in liquid form but have added flavoring that may not be appealing to kids. Compounding works on these medications, too.

Ask your doctor and pharmacist about custom mixing a compound that your child will take. A compounding pharmacist can even make medication into lollipops or candy and give you a choice of two or three flavors. The consistency of the medication can be changed (think to thin, thin to thick) and it can also be concentrated so you don't have to give such a large quantity.

You want to remember that compounded medications may lose their potency after a few weeks, so ask your pharmacist for advice. You can consult with the International Association of Compounding Pharmacists for detailed information on compounding and flavoring medications.

PILLS AND CAPSULES

Medications come in a variety of forms including tablets, encapsulated capsules, buffered tablets and micro-encapsulated (melt-in-your-mouth) tablets, micro-encapsulated packets (powder to mix in water) and an actual powder. Some even come in IV forms.

Advice from a GERD Mom...

My four year old just started taking a new dissolving tablet. I told her we were going try a new medicine that was magic. So we made up a little routine: you put it in your mouth and then mommy will count to 10 and it will disappear on your tongue. She loves opening her mouth to say, "Ta Da!" when it is all gone. Of course I made a huge deal about the magic for the first two weeks or so and made a point of saying to anyone that happened to be there (i.e. dad, grandparents),"Watch we have a special magic trick you won't believe." My daughter is very dramatic so I indulge that side of her by making a huge production out of things when I need her cooperation and it works really well for us!

If a medication comes in a pill or capsule form, do not crush the pill or open the capsule unless given specific instructions by the pharmacist. Do not cut tablets that are not "scored" with an indented line. Crushing, splitting or opening pills and capsules may ruin the effectiveness of the medication, especially a time-released medication such as a Proton Pump Inhibitor (PPI).

Your pharmacist or doctor can call the manufacturer to learn how to give these medicines without inactivating them. The instructions may be different for each form and each brand. By carefully follow instructions from your doctor or pharmacist when giving pills or capsules to your child, you won't mistakenly compromise the medicine's effectiveness.

What your child drinks to get that pill or capsule down can also adversely affect the effectiveness of the medication. Double check with the pharmacist about the formula or other foods/drinks your child is likely to use to take her medication. For instance, grapefruit juice should never be taken with any medication.

> ## A GERD Mom Says...
>
> I looked at the capsule filled with little beads and I looked at my infant daughter. Now how in the world was I supposed to get this medication into her?! I called the pharmacist and found out how to mix the beads in her baby food.

Another issue in giving medications is timing. Some medicines can't be mixed with each other and should be given at different times of day. Again, your doctor or pharmacist can review your child's medications and properly coordinate the times they are given.

A few medicines come in a dissolving form such as an efferdose tablet that dissolves in your mouth. Some of these efferdose tablets can be dissolved in water and the liquid can then be drawn into an oral syringe and given to an infant.

12 ►HIGH NEED PARENTING

You may have a hard time remembering what you did before you had children. Perhaps you had a career and a job you enjoyed. Now it may seem like caretaking is your career. You are on call 24/7: feeding, comforting, mixing medication and formula, cleaning up spit, trotting to doctors appointments, negotiating with your insurance company…the list goes on. The pay is awful and the hours are long. How did this happen to you?

Your back aches and you are constantly in a state of exhaustion. You can't remember the last time you slept in your bed, much less had a full nights sleep. You seldom get a break from your role. You don't have any control over your life, your job and your other family responsibilities. Will it every end?

Day in and day out, you perform the same jobs over and over, wash, clean, feed, start over…you know intuitively that you are doing the most important job you can do. You love your child more than anything and that is

> ## *Jan says:*
>
> Before my daughter Rebecca was born, I worked with infants and toddlers with severe developmental delays, helping parents develop caretaking routines for play, eating and sleep. Nothing prepared me for the intensive care giving required in parenting a high need baby with medical problems. I have spoken with medical experts—MD's and PhD's who have a child with GERD—and they all say the same thing: parenting their child with reflux has been the hardest thing they have ever done.

usually enough to get you though a hard day on the job. You get paid in hugs and kisses. Who could ask for more?

Each day is so busy that you may not think about your life too much. You may experience times when you can't look at the future and you may feel it is best to just take one step at a time; solve the problem in front of you at the moment and don't worry too much about next week or next year.

This chapter will address the special caretaking issues facing parents who find that reflux lasts longer than expected or is more severe than the typical case. Think of it as a virtual support group. You will hear the voices of other parents who share your fears and isolation. When reading this, you may feel reassured to find that others share your struggles. If it is too depressing, skip ahead to the "Top 10 Coping Tips" for some parent tested ways to cope with caring for your baby with GERD.

Feelings

You may feel that the initial joy and euphoria from childbirth has been quickly replaced with a dark cloud of frustration, anxiety and exhaustion. This may happen in the hospital if your baby has reflux symptoms immediately or it may unfold as the days and week's progress and your baby begins to experience pain and discomfort from eating.

We all read the baby books while we were pregnant so we knew that sleep deprivation and care taking were part of the parenting package deal. We read that babies cry, spit up, mess their diapers and do other unpleasant things. We also read that we would bond with our babies and love every minute of feeding and hugging.

So what happened? While the other moms were dressing their babies in Baby Gap matching outfits and meeting friends for lunch at the coffee shop, we ended up at home, in formula and spit up stained clothes, holding a fussy baby with tears streaming down our cheeks. The other moms got tickets to the "Parenting by the Book Tour" while you get to ride on the "Reflux Rollercoaster."

Don't worry, you are not alone. Your feelings are very normal and expected under the circumstances. You will find other companions on your journey. Somewhere in the distant future, you may even be surprised to hear yourself say, "It was hard but I am glad I did it."

DISAPPOINTED

You may feel disappointed that your plans to be a super mom with a perfect baby have been replaced by the grim realities of smelly vomit covered clothes and deep lines of stress and fatigue on your face.

> ### A GERD Mom Says...
>
> When he turned 6 months of age, I was a little disappointed that he hadn't outgrown his reflux. I was sure he would outgrow it by one year of age. At his one year old birthday, he wouldn't even eat his cake because he is a picky eater and only tolerates pureed food. I felt so sad and depressed. I felt so cheated. When would the reflux ever end? I felt depressed for weeks after his birthday.

You may feel disappointed when several months go by and she still has reflux. Sometimes, the doctor will tell you the baby will outgrow the reflux when she sits up or by one year of age. As parents, we mark our calendars, waiting for the reflux to go away! But then it doesn't end and we wonder if we can keep our strength and commitment up until it does end.

GUILT

You may look back on the pregnancy and delivery for clues about what you did to "cause" the problem. Did I eat too much acidic food? Was it the medication at childbirth? Is there something wrong with my milk? Don't go there. There is no medical evidence to support such an assumption so don't get ahead of the facts.

Then there is the "why me?" reaction; you're not alone. You will feel this way and you will get beyond those feelings. Just as you are patient with your child, be patient with yourself.

OVERWHELMED

When you entered the world of parenting, you knew that you would be busy taking care of your little bundle of joy and would learn a whole new genre of meaning, from rear facing car seat to diaper rash. What you didn't expect was getting a whole medical education, adding fancy terms to your vocabulary such as pediatric gastroenterologist and gastroesophageal reflux. Just when you had mastered

A GERD Mom Says...

I got pregnant when my older daughter was only 8 months old. I sometimes feel a little bad because all the happiness and joy we had with my older daughter is pretty much gone. Our time is spent in doctor's offices, hospitals and pacing the floor with a crying infant. I look at our happy toddler and feel tremendous guilt about what we can't give her in terms of our time. We used to laugh and play. Now we just try to get through the day with our sanity intact. My husband and I get short with each other a lot because we are both just so tired of being tired. Don't get me wrong, we love our new baby so much, but it does make me long for the one-on-one time with our other daughter. The joy we so longed for in becoming parents was short lived. Now each day is long and exhausting with very little fun.

breastfeeding and umbilical cord care, you had to learn to measure medications, modify your diet and learn 27 ways to burp and soothe a very unhappy little baby.

Taking care of a fussy, unhappy baby can consume most of your time, making it difficult if not impossible to take care of *your* basic needs such as eating, sleeping and bathing. The house is a mess, the bills haven't been paid and you can't imagine how you will find the time to go to the grocery store.

EXHAUSTED

Your whole body may ache from holding and carrying your inconsolable infant or clingy toddler. It is hard work to bend and lift, vacuum and load the washing machine with a baby on your shoulder or in a carrier. You may be in a state of exhaustion from a full day of caretaking only to face frequent night waking for more feeding, holding and comforting. Most of the night duty falls on the shoulders of mothers, especially breastfeeding moms—even with the help of a supportive spouse. The nights can feel very long.

What about "sleep when the baby sleeps"?

My 10 week old baby didn't even take a nap during the day. Occasionally, she would pass out for 15-20 minutes after a really bad crying spell. She seldom slept more than 2 or 3 hours at night before waking up again. How was I supposed to "sleep when the baby sleeps" if she was wide awake all day?

So, what is happening to you? What happened to the happy, funny woman you used to be? The long term consequences of interrupted sleep can include mental confusion, depression and moodiness. You may also have a difficult time focusing and remembering things. Some sleep deprived parents find that they get angry or upset easily.

Everyone tells you to "sleep when the baby sleeps" this advice works just grand if you only have one baby, if you have live in staff including a housekeeper, nanny and cook, and you don't work outside the home. Ok, so that is not you. Instead, what you do is take a shower, pay the bills or throw in a load of laundry the moment you get the baby peeled off your shoulder. You are positively joyful about being able to move faster and bend over without whacking her in the head as you get some basic chores done.

MISUNDERSTOOD

Doesn't it seem like every time you complain to the doctor about how much your baby is crying, there she is, sleeping through the entire appointment? And grandma has heard you carry on about your picky eater...only now that grandma is here, she won't keep her hand out of the snack bowl!

You just want to scream if one more person tells you, "she looks so healthy", "she will eat when she is hungry" or "my child did the same thing." Welcome...you are joining the ranks of GERD parents who say, "you should have seen her [yesterday], [a minute ago], [last night]..."!

ANGER AND FRUSTRATION

You may feel anger toward those you love and need most: your spouse, your family and your friends. You may even feel angry at your baby. You have no control over your life. Everything is too hard. No one understands. You may find yourself lashing out at anyone in your path.

A GERD Mom's Experience...

One night she kept waking up every 30-45 minutes. I would nurse her and she would fall asleep on my chest. Every time I placed her back in her crib, she would instantly wake up and start crying again. This went on for about 3 hours. I felt my anger rising. I was losing control. I was so tired, I just couldn't function another minute. I woke up my husband and asked him to hold her. I didn't tell him, but at that moment I felt like I could hurt her.

ISOLATED

None of the other moms in the moms club have an inconsolable baby who spits and arches. Your relatives tell you no other family member acted like this during infancy; all the other grand babies ate and slept just fine. You feel like the only parent in the history of the universe to have such a difficult baby. You cannot face going to the moms club or sharing your story with other parents. They just don't seem to get it.

STRESSED AND ANXIOUS

Parenting a child with reflux can cause plenty of stress: financial, marital and personal. Reflux affects every aspect of your lives. You may be on extended leave from work at a time when your medical bills are very high. You may feel angry and unsupported by your spouse. Your spouse may be disappointed that he/she has lost your attention at a time when intimacy is the last thing on your mind.

When you are overloaded with demands and worried about finances and family matters, it is common to feel anxious and stressed. You worry about the little things and the big things; you worry about how you will get through this day and how the story will end; you worry about worrying!

A WORD ABOUT SHAKEN BABY SYNDROME

Sometimes a baby can make you feel a level of anger you never thought was possible. Fatigue and frustration can build up and in a moment of rage, the baby may become the focus of your anger. Parents have been known to shake or smack a baby in an attempt to stop the crying. Shaking a baby can cause permanent eye or brain damage and even death because a young baby does not have the head/neck control to withstand the force of the motion.

If you feel that your anger is rising to a dangerous level, you need to take immediate action:

✓ Put your baby in a safe place, such as a baby seat or crib, and go to another room so you cannot hear the crying.

✓ Call someone—a spouse, friend or neighbor—to come over right away.

✓ Seek medical care; perhaps your baby is crying due to illness.

✓ Put the baby in a car seat and drive; perhaps the car ride will be soothing.

DEPRESSED

Some mothers suffer from severe hormone swings after their baby is born and these hormone swings can keep you dwelling on negative issues. It can take a year for a new mother's hormones to level out and you may be more prone to tears and self-criticism during this time. If you find that negative thoughts are interfering with doing what needs to be done, it may be a signal to seek help. Taking care of a baby with reflux is challenging and this type of stress can tip the baby blues into full-blown postpartum depression.

It is actually well documented that mothers of babies with 'severe colic' are much more likely to become depressed. Most people don't realize that postpartum depression can be VERY serious. Some women get so confused that they hallucinate. If you feel yourself losing your grip, talk to friends, your family and your doctor about your difficulties. The bottom line is you need to take care of yourself so that you can take care of your baby.

Top Ten Coping Tips

Surviving day to day may seem challenging but, with these parent-tested and approved strategies, it is possible to get by. So, from the hundreds of parents who have spent innumerable years taking care of babies and children with reflux, here are my top ten tips for coping.

Teamwork: A strong parenting team will work together, share the responsibilities and give each other support and a break.

Second Shift: Find a babysitter, friend or relative to give both parents a break.

Take care of yourself: Take a break, take a shower, chew your food, and drink your water.

Care giver Routine: Pace yourself, develop a schedule.

Trust your instincts: Trust your instincts and avoid unhelpful, bossy people.

Let go of other responsibilities: No need to be superwoman or supermom any more.

Live in the present tense.

Network: Develop a support network.

Humor: an often underrated coping technique!

Celebrate this child!

Now, let's go into these tips in more depth.

TEAMWORK

It is time to mobilize TEAM REFLUX! You and your spouse/partner need to form a strong parenting team. Remember, the key to teamwork is communicating often and expressing wants and needs. It is everyone's responsibility to

listen carefully, acknowledge feelings and needs. While it is
easy to blame the other parent and put up a wall of anger, it

---

Here's an Idea...

Sometimes I had to give my husband a big hint that I needed
help. I would say, in a gentle voice, "If you want dinner, come
home 30 minutes before you are hungry!" With 3 children
under the age of 5, this was neither a joke nor a threat.

My husband would come in the door and corral the kids. I
headed for the kitchen to make a quick meal. I would turn on
the radio, sip a bit of wine and get the food on the table.   By
working as a team, we had a real dinner once in a while.

---

will do little to help the situation. You both need to develop a
plan, work together and support each others efforts.

SECOND SHIFT

Even Team Reflux needs a second shift. Sometimes the job
is too big for two parents...much less one! You may find that
there is a need for an additional adult to help with the
household and the baby.

A GERD Mom Says...

My parents came to stay with us after another tearful phone
call about how hard it was to take care of Sara. They came in
and immediately rolled up their sleeves and helped us in so
many ways: shopping, rocking the baby and making meals.
Within a week THEY were on the brink of exhaustion and
called a nanny agency to hire a full time care giver. It took 5
adults to take care of one little baby!

Some parents find that they need to take care of the baby
   because no one else can manage the feeding and the
   comforting. So, how about getting someone to take care of
   what you cannot?
Others find that they like a break from the care giving. You
   would be surprised how tolerant another adult can be with a
   crying baby—as long as they get to go home at the end of the
   day!

If someone offers to make a hot meal, run to the store, vacuum, do dishes, pick-up and drop-off of the siblings...accept! This is the time to let others reach out to you with their practical expression of caring and concern. When this phase of your life is over, you can return the favor for someone else.

TAKE CARE OF YOURSELF

This seems like such a cliché. When no one but you can calm the baby or keep the milk from "urping up," how are you supposed to take a break? Of course you would love a break but who is going to take over? You are still waiting for Mary Poppins to appear at your door.

> ### A GERD Mom Says...
>
> I try to take a walk with my baby every day. I think she feels better when we go outside for a walk either in the sling or in the stroller. It is a change of pace and feels good for both of us.

Everyone says, "take some time to do what you enjoy...read a book or go out to eat." That doesn't feel helpful when you are happy just to take a shower and chew your food. You don't even know what day of the week it is much less what book is on the best sellers list.

Try to do something little, something symbolic. It can be something as simple as sitting at the table rather than standing at the counter while you eat and write out the bills while on hold with the doctor's office.

Take your vitamins, eat well, and maintain your own health. It is surprising how something as little as drinking enough water during the day can provide more energy and balance. Find a way to get a bit of exercise. Even if you have to exercise with your baby attached to you. It is hard work. But remember, you are the most important person in the world to your baby and he/she needs you to stay healthy and well.

CARE GIVER ROUTINE

Taking care of a baby with reflux is like running a marathon. You need to pace yourself and save some energy for the last miles. As much as possible, develop a schedule. It is likely that a schedule will help you feel more in control and will help your baby feel more settled, too.

Know, too, that there will be days when you will need to abandon your schedule and just do what needs to be done. Let

---

What Other GERD Parents Do:

Every afternoon at 4pm the crying would start. And just about every afternoon, I would place Maggie in the stroller and headed up the street. Everyone could hear the wailing as we passed. Before long, a neighbor or two would stop to say hello or join me on the walk. It became a bit of a joke-everyone knew we were coming from a mile away since Maggie was so noisy!

◆

I would not say that we had a routine for the day; it was more like a rhythm. It helped me as much as it helped my daughter. At sun up, it was time to eat breakfast. Before lunch, we always took a walk. After lunch was time to nap. When my husband came home, I took a few minutes to be alone or complete a task without interruption. After dinner was bath and rocking time before bed.

---

it happen, and then pull yourself and your baby back into the schedule.

Consider, too, that your schedule lets others know when you're "available" and they can stop in to visit or give you a call. You'd be amazed how refreshing you will find those few minutes of "adult time."

TRUSTING YOUR INSTINCTS

Go ahead, trust your instincts. Go with your gut. Hear your inner voice. You are an expert on your child. You know what is best for him/her. Surround yourself with people who know you and care about you. Confide in those who value your opinion and support your decisions.

HUMOR

Having a baby with reflux may not seem funny but sometimes, you just have to laugh. Otherwise, you will end up crying or feeling angry. There is nothing like viewing your life from an eagle's perch and seeing the humor. Can't quite see the humor? If you have a trusted friend with a good sense of humor, tell her some stories and let her find the humor. Let yourself laugh with her and feel some of those knots of tension untie.

From a Veteran Reflux Mom...

I'm pretty sure I hold the world record for paying for vomit. During the pre-holiday rush, I took my infant son, David, food shopping despite the risks involved. My son is a champion spitter and can cover a car seat, freshly laundered clothes and carpeting in no time. Things were going pretty well until we got to the produce section. Before you could say Brussels sprouts, David had managed to vomit into a bag of fresh, ripe pears!

I am a veteran reflux mom and I had dealt with my share of reflux emergencies so I knew just what to do. I simply put the messy bag of pears in the cart and proceeded to the checkout. The clerk raised the bag of pears onto the scale and said, "Ma'am, there's something wrong with the pears. Do you want to get some new ones?" I calmly said, "Its o.k. My son vomited into the bag." So the clerk weighed the pears, plus goo, and sent us on our way, leaving a few bemused shoppers in line.

LET GO OF OTHER RESPONSIBILITIES

It may seem like there are too many items on the "TO DO" list and you are falling hopelessly behind. You never get anything crossed off and more items are added daily. It is time to take a good hard look at your responsibilities and decide what really needs to be done. Taking care of the baby, eating and sleeping may be all you keep on the list. Remember, this is a time of intensive parenting; you have a child who needs you more than anything else. Eventually, this season will end and she will grow and feel better.

LIVE IN THE PRESENT TENSE

Caretakers are champions in multi-tasking; you can read a picture book while planning dinner and remembering to call the refill in to the pharmacy. We all need a break from the stress this pressure causes. Living in the present tense means letting go of "forward looking" and instead focus on the moment you are experiencing now.

Put all your energy into that moment. Look at where you are, what you are doing. Clear your head; focus on your book, on your child, and on your closeness to each other. Smell the sweetness of her hair, feel the closeness and relaxation you both feel.

There…now you are living in the present.

NETWORK

Several studies show that patients and families, who develop a network of support through a patient support group or organization, have better medical outcomes than those who do not seek information. Many of the feelings experienced by parents caring for their child with reflux can be shared with…and accepted by…other parents experiencing the same joys and challenges.

> ### *Jan says:*
>
> Before I found other reflux moms, I felt very isolated and frustrated. I searched everywhere for patient information and only came across books about adults with reflux. Even though I had wonderful doctors and a supportive family, I still needed to speak to other parents. It was a powerful experience to actually talk with someone who understood; I felt empowered to try new treatments and have a positive outlook on the situation.

143

Parent-to-parent networking is possible, especially on-line. In this virtual community, you can participate in discussion forums or chat groups, post messages, vent, ask questions and share ideas.

CELEBRATE THIS CHILD

By now, many of you may have thrown out the parenting books and the hand-me-down rule book telling you how you are *supposed* to raise this child with reflux. Next, consider throwing out your worry and stress and take a good look at your child. Celebrate who she is; focus on her beautiful little body, her warm, smooth skin, her little nose that looks like Uncle Fred's. Take pictures of her. How about a picture of her finally falling asleep on dad's shoulder (notice that dad is asleep too!) or crying in Grandma's arms. Perhaps you can't take a picture of her actually eating cake on her first birthday. Go ahead and take a picture of her anyway with her cute outfit and party hat.

Common Parent Concerns

We can all imagine the worst; it is much too easy. Other times our concerns seem embarrassingly trivial, but we're not sure; maybe they are reasonable and important. Up and down the emotional roller coaster we go. Am I the only one who thinks crazy thoughts, who finds feelings and experiences larger than life? If you share those feelings, thoughts, experiences you might find out that you are not alone. Here are some concerns other parents have shared.

IT SEEMS THIS WILL GO ON FOREVER

Caring for a baby or child with GERD makes it highly likely you will have setbacks and problems along the way. It may seem that the reflux is getting better and then a new tooth erupts or your little one catches the cough that is going around...and back to square one. Remember, it took a while to get into this situation; it will take some time and patience to get out.

> ### A GERD Mom Says...
>
> My doctor said that it can take many months being out of pain until her sleep problems will be fully gone. It is already much better but we have a way to go.

I CAN'T THINK CLEARLY

Daytime parenting is an exercise in patience and stamina, even on a good day. Then there are your child's reflux episodes at night and you may have your endurance tested further. No question, after a full day of caretaking you really deserve a good night's sleep. Your aching body is crying for rest and your brain cannot process another shred of information. Your whole being needs to rest. Then, just as you are placing your head on your pillow, there is a familiar sound. Your baby is crying, no, shrieking...again. You are a parent and so you are instantly awake.

As a parent, you don't need a sleep deprivation study to tell you what you already know. Not getting enough sleep leaves you feeling drained and tired all day. You may also feel like your brain doesn't work and you can't think clearly, even for the simplest task. Adults who do not get enough sleep are at risk for illness, accidents and poor job performance.

We know this and we also know that along with the expertise in multi-tasking, a care giver of a child with reflux will become very adept at making decisions when tired...even beyond tired. If you are worried about your decision making ability or your instincts tell you something is going wrong, time to call in Team Reflux! Maybe your wonderful neighbor will come over and walk the screaming baby for a few hours while you take a break.

> ### A GERD Mom Says ...
>
> The sound of her crying pierces my body and wakes my brain from a deep sleep. She is awake again. I check the clock and notice that I just got into bed an hour ago; time to start the night shift.

I FEEL ANGRY AND FRUSTRATED

Sleep deprivation may change the way you react to problems large and small. You may have less patience and a higher anger quotient. A little problem may seem huge. The first person you see in the day—your spouse, the garbage man, the doctor—may be the recipient of your misplaced anger just by being in the wrong place at the wrong time. Alone in the dark night, you may feel exhausted and angry at your baby for waking you up again.

Veteran parents of GERD children know that this is normal; they know they will get through this without permanently alienating everyone they know. Jump back in this chapter and read the section on "Feelings." Take a deep breath and then read the "Top 10 Tips."

I AM AFRAID MY BABY WILL CHOKE AT NIGHT

Some babies seem to choke, cough and hold their breath during and after a feeding (see chapter on "Symptoms"). If your baby has shown actual signs of being in distress, of course you are going to be on high alert day and night. How could you NOT worry? What is any doctor or grandparent going to tell you that will make you feel less worried? Your parenting instincts are telling you something is wrong and you have to stay nearby night and day.

So how are your supposed to sleep? Your brain tells you to stay awake but your body is craving sleep. You train your brain and your body to "hear" in your sleep and wake up at the slightest change of breathing or a twig falling on the roof.

AM I SPOILING MY BABY?

You may have been told that you are spoiling the baby by holding her all day; that she will never be able to sooth herself or play independently. Someone may have told you that rocking your baby to sleep and sleeping with her at night will make her clingy and dependent as a toddler and beyond. Then there are the "baby trainers" out there instructing parents on how to train the baby to eat, sleep and behave. Books and videos teach parents special techniques to calm and train their baby. Unfortunately, baby training does not work when an infant or child is experiencing chronic pain and discomfort.

While you work to manage the pain that is preventing her from learning how to self-sooth, you can still develop routines to increase her independence for play and sleep. For instance, you can help her to associate a blanket, stuffed animal or music box with calming and going to sleep as you are rocking her. Over time, you can gradually rock her for a shorter period of time and put her in bed with her familiar objects and music when she is still awake.

When you know the GERD is under control or your child has outgrown the reflux, you may need to help her learn self-soothing and greater independence for sleeping. Some parents find that they are comfortable with a more intensive method of developing independence for sleep. These approaches often have dramatic results in a short period of time. The trick is to know whether the reflux is really under control and when to try a particular method. When you and the doctor are sure that she is not experiencing pain at night from reflux, you can gently teach her to self-calm and stay asleep all night long.

I Can't Believe Letting Her Cry is Right!

If your baby woke up every two hours due to pain from an ear infection, would family and friends advise you to let her cry it out at night? Most likely the answer would be no. So why do family, friends and even physicians tell you that it is ok to let your little one cry it out when she wakes up at night due to painful reflux episodes?

When reflux is causing the night waking, letting her

> ### *Jan says:*
>
> When my daughter was about 15 months old, I read a book about teaching your baby to sleep. I tried the techniques a few nights. I would go into her room and place her back down in the crib and talk soothingly before leaving the room. Of course she continued to cry. It was just awful for both of us. I finally stopped when I walked into her room the next day and saw the big puddle of spit- up on her sheets and on the floor. She became so upset that she vomited.

cry it out just won't work. Everyone needs to remember that, in time, the reflux will get better and she will learn to sleep because the pain doesn't jerk her awake or keep her awake.

Family Issues

Naturally enough, when people talk about the impact of having a baby with reflux, they focus on the baby's care giver (most often the moms). In reality, reflux affects the whole

> ### *A Reflux Dad Says...*
>
> I know it has been hard on my wife, caring for our son with reflux. He takes a lot of her time and energy. I try to help as much as I can. I know my wife loves me and I appreciate what she does, but I miss spending time alone with her. I don't think our lack of private time bothers her nearly as much as it bothers me.

family. Dads, siblings and grandparents all feel many of the strong emotions experienced by mom, including frustration, confusion and exhaustion.

The way we deal with health issues depends on our parenting styles, our perception of our role and how we deal with stress. It is important to recognize that our concerns and coping styles may clash with those around us during a health care crisis. For instance, you may have mourned the loss of the perfect baby while your spouse has not. Grandma may be in denial while you are feeling anger and disappointment. Understanding these patterns may help you understand why people act the way they do.

DADS

It may seem that only mom can take care of the baby. Dads often get left out of caretaking and the mom becomes the expert. In addition, mothers may get all of the sympathy and support even though dads may be just as disappointed, worried and stressed as mom. As it turns out, Dads often want the same thing as moms.

A Helping Hand...

I was too busy to get on the computer so my husband sat down and did some research on reflux. It made him feel good to have an actual job to do and he learned that all of the reflux moms on the discussion boards sounded just as worn out as his wife!!!

Moms and Dads have similar needs. It is important for parents to nurture each other and communicate their needs during this difficult time. Moms and dads need to give each other space to develop their own parenting style and respect each other's parenting decisions too. Dads may want a turn with caretaking activities such as feeding, bathing and diapering. Moms often want assistance with these tasks. Work on these few but essential components to taking care of Dad and your relationship.

Communication: Moms and dads need to communicate clearly and frequently about their concerns. Mom wants to talk about her day, her long night, and her fears. Dad may be focused on the finances and earning a living.

Encouragement and positive feedback: Dad needs to hear some positive words, from mom such as, "Thank you, it was nice to have a break." "You are doing a good job." "The baby likes it when you do that." Dads also need to remember that

---

From Jan's blog at www.healthcentral.com:

Presumably there are just as many reflux dads as there are reflux moms. On a day to day basis, I tend to hear from many more reflux moms. I know the dads are out there but I get the feeling most of them lurk on the message board rather than leave a message. The reflux dads I talk with share the same concerns and often have the same questions as moms: Will the reflux get better? What are the treatment options? How do we get our baby to sleep at night?

Mom needs to hear your positive feedback as well. Your positive attitude and kind words will make her day!

A break: Mom needs a nap and a break from the baby. Guess what? Dad needs some downtime too. It is important to communicate these needs and have a coordinated approach. Go back in this chapter and read "Teamwork." It's all about Team Reflux.

Adult time: Dad misses the old days when he had your full attention. Parenting decreases the amount of 'couples' time. Parenting a child with GERD might bring this necessary time down to mere minutes each day. Try to make the most of those precious minutes.

GRANDPARENTS

Grandparents feel a deep connection and bond to their grandchildren. So it makes sense that they may experience a high level of anxiety and fear about an illness that affects their grandchild. Grandparents want to fix the problem affecting their precious grandchild and they want to help you, too.

Remember, you are always the child in the eyes of your parents and they want to kiss the hurts and offer hugs for the disappointment.

Unfortunately, when everyone is stressed and worried, communication may break down and attempts to help might make the situation worse. That is why some parents feel the grandparents are meddling when they attempt to give advice, help with the chores or call their golf partner who is a pediatrician.

Another point of conflict is often the baby's fussiness and chronic crying or the parent's ready response to a whiny toddler. In the past, parents were instructed to not indulge fussing and whining. They were expected to let their fussy babies cry it out so they would not get spoiled. If the baby was really fussy or the mother was hysterical and exhausted, mom or baby might have been offered sedation or sleeping pills. Grandparents may need to be educated about new approaches to soothing a child in pain.

A GERD Mom's Story:

A few months after my daughter was born, I was leafing through my baby book. I came across a prescription that had been taped into the book. My mom said that I had been a fussy baby and the doctor prescribed a strong sedative for me. She never filled it because she didn't see how sedating me was going to take care of my pain.

On the other hand, grandma or grandpa may be more patient than you are when it comes to walking a fussy baby back and forth across the room for hours on end. They may see a new way to calm and sooth their grandchild. It's all about trial and error and putting more than one or two brains on the problem could be a big help.

BROTHERS AND SISTERS

You look in the mirror and reflected back is someone you don't recognize: drawn, red eyed with frown lines and hair badly in need of a good cut. You look down and reflected, standing next to you, is your child without GERD and you see sad or frightened eyes, a thumb being sucked, a mouth not smiling. It pierces your heart.

Children absorb the atmosphere of their home like sponges. Your children without GER or GERD may feel concern about their sick brother or sister. They may think it is their fault or that the baby is going to die. All of those urgent phone calls and sudden trips to the hospital combined with one look at your worried face is all they need to think the worse.

You're stressed; Dad's stressed; and your baby's siblings are stressed, too. Their stress can show up in many ways, almost none of them involving words. Some kids deal with stress by being as helpful as they can be, like a little adult. Other children take out their anger and frustration by reverting to an old pattern of behavior (having potty accidents) or acting out (emptying the flour on the kitchen floor while you are cleaning vomit off the couch).

Ideas for helping brothers and sisters include:

Routine: Stick to a routine as much as possible. It will help them feel safe and secure.

Parent Time: Schedule one-to-one parent time; read a story, spend a few minutes on the swing or pick any other activity that involves just you and him.

Inclusion: Brothers and sisters often want to help. Let them. Simple care giving tasks that they can complete successfully will make them feel involved, acknowledging that they are part of Team Reflux, too.

Listen and Communicate: Give her permission to express her needs and concerns to you. You might have to help a young child find the words to express what they feel by role modeling and using words they can understand. It is important to see the world from their point of view.

152

Bring out the art supplies: Often children will express themselves using pictures or stories. Share their artwork or their story with them; talk about what *they* want to tell you about their creative work.

A GERD Mom's Experience...

Hanna came home from preschool with a picture titled My Family. There was baby Rachel all snug between mom and dad in the middle of the picture. Hanna was pictured playing by herself in the corner. I could see that she felt small, left out and alone.

Understand their side: Taking a walk in someone else's shoes was never more important than now. Try to see the world from the sibling's point of view. He needs your overworked brain to focus on how he's experiencing this difficult time.

Bringing in the Professionals: When to Seek Counseling

Don't expect that you can cope with everything just fine, and then one day find yourself unable to get out of bed. Caring for a child with a chronic illness can leave you feeling angry, depressed, and guilty. It can affect your marriage and your relationship with your children, your parents or your friends. It is important for you to get the support and assistance that you need. You are worth it and your family is definitely worth it.

A parent support group may provide the emotional support and companionship you need. Definitely try that and see if it does work. However, do not hesitate to call in the professionals if support is not enough.

When you do seek counseling, get a referral to a counselor who specializes in working with patients who are dealing with chronic illness. There are many avenues you can use to find the professional you need. You may want to talk with your physician. You can contact the psychological association in

153

your state; many can provide names of counselors in your area for your specific need. Turn to other parents caring for children with GERD, either online or in town for a recommendation.

Speak with each possible professional. Ask them questions about their expertise and how they work with their patients. Talk about what you need and how much time you can spend. Remember that counseling can take many forms. Marriage counseling, family counseling or individual counseling; any one or all of these may be a positive step toward coping with the stress created by your intensive level of care giving.

It isn't just your family that needs you to cope with the stress and feelings you have as a care giver. Your health is also at risk; we now know that

> ### *It Does Help...*
>
> ...to talk to someone professionally, like a counselor. I finally did when my daughter was 15 months and I wish I had done it from day one. I am still hyper and over-reactive at times about things. That only gets better with time and as your child starts to age and you feel like the reflux is getting more manageable.

stress is a contributing factor to chronic illness and disease. Take care of yourself and you will be better able to take care of those who love and depend on you.

Dealing with Advice from Others

We've touched on the well-meaning advice you get from family and friends: "Let him cry it out"; "All babies will eat when they are good and hungry"; "You are spoiling him by holding him all of the time"; "She will never learn to sleep in her crib if you keep taking her into your bed." Normally, you would just take these comments in stride. However, at the moment, you are in no mood for unsolicited advice or judgment of your parenting decisions. You are too stressed and sleep deprived to educate and explain about why you do what you do.

People just can't hold back from giving advice to parents. From friends and relatives to total strangers, everyone has something to say. Advice on eating and sleeping seem to be favorite topics, too.

You may feel as if you will have a temper tantrum every time someone makes a comment or gives a tidbit of advice. While the comments are well meaning, they seem to de-value your parenting and lead to self doubt and confusion. So how do you respond to all that advice when coping is not something you're doing well right at the moment?

Here are other parents' ideas for dealing with advice.

One sentence explanation: Have a short explanation for your child's issues such as, "She is crying because of the reflux."

Refrain from commenting. You do not have to comment, agree or disagree.

Find a circle of support: Find a friend or support group and share your feelings in a safe environment.

Quote the doctor: For instance, "The doctor said she needs to be held most of the time."

On line chat/support group: Use the internet to find others for a virtual support group.

Humor: Don't take the advice too seriously. Use humor to respond to comments.

Taking Care of the Caretaker: You

As a typical care giver of a child with GERD, you spend every waking moment precisely following the doctor's home treatment, then driving in circles between the clinic and the pharmacy. Odds are you are neglecting your own health care needs and perhaps putting your health and well being in jeopardy.

TAKING THE FIRST STEP

It's been a hard day and your neighbor stops you for a visit when you're on the way to the mailbox. Maybe you have lost weight and skipped the hair appointment (now that you have quit your job and you are living paycheck to paycheck). She may comment on how tired and rundown you look. When you try to respond, it may just be too difficult to explain that you just spent an hour on the phone fighting with the insurance company. While you're formulating an answer, she gives you some more of the well meaning advice you've been getting from others lately:

"Take care of yourself."

"Eat healthy foods."

"Go out and have lunch with a friend."

"Get some exercise."

"Take on a hobby."

It is kind that people notice the toll it takes on you, caring for a child with a chronic illness. However, their attempts to offer advice may not be welcome and may even make you feel angry. You may feel that these "advisors" obviously have no real understanding of your life. Sure you would like to go out every week with your co-workers but you are barely holding things together and the effort to go out may seem too exhausting. You know the weekly girl's night out group has gone on without you week after week.

With all these conflicting demands and desires, your response to this well-meaning advice may be terse and even cold. To an outsider, your mood at that moment could be misconstrued as "who you are" all of the time; they don't know its exhaustion talking, not you.

Rather than chastise yourself or your neighbor for insensitivity, take this exchange as a signal: could taking care of yourself not just slipped a bit, but dropped over the edge? Taking care of *you* begins by doing one simple thing. It can be anything, anything that gets you moving toward better mental, emotional and physical health. Here are a few to get you started.

Take a multi vitamin each day.

Drink your water...all 36 ounces of it.

Take an extra long shower.

Take your friend up on her offer to watch the baby and take a nice, long walk.

Add one healthy food to your diet.

Keep a list next to your phone of things other people can do to help when they call and ask.

Each time you do something for your own health and well being, tell yourself, "I am important. I am doing important work and I need to be healthy for my family. They are counting on me."

DON'T GO IT ALONE

You may feel lonely at times as you take care of a child with a chronic illness 24/7. It is a long journey, seemingly

Jan says:

Nurse Joan noticed that we had a lot in common; we both had girls with severe reflux and needed to spend the night in the hospital for a pH probe. So Joan assigned us to the same room in the pediatric ward. The other mom, Jessica, and I stayed up half the night talking about our kids, our frustrations and our fears-it was like a slumber party for moms with sick kids! Five years later, Jessica and I still talk on the phone frequently and our children are very close. Jessica is my lifeline. I know I can call her about anything. Only another mom could understand what I am talking about and not judge me or get bored with my endless worries and stories. When I go to the specialist or have a really hard day, I always call Jessica. She keeps me going!

endless. It is highly recommended that you find someone to travel that difficult road with you. Some of you are blessed to have a supportive spouse and family to listen and share the work. You may also be lucky enough to find a friend who truly understands and willingly walks at your side. Or, you may find your traveling companions in your internet support network. Wherever and whomever you turn to, their companionship and support is vital to your health and well being.

BALANCE

It may seem totally impossible to balance everything. Just when you feel like you are getting a tiny bit ahead, something else happens. Staying balanced, providing yourself with time for *you* may seem like a dream.   Every day is spent looking ahead, anticipating what your child will need, and planning for the next step in the treatment plan. Living in the present may seem not only impossible, but counterproductive, too.

Yet, it is by living in the present tense that we can gain a sense of control and balance. How you do this is as different as you are from anyone else.   You may find your balance by surrounding yourself with supportive people. Others may find they need to simplify by lowering their expectations for now or putting off things they want or should do. Maybe you can find balance by putting a little fun in your life; more laughter, more playing. What ever works for you and however you find it, the important thing is searching for your balance and maintaining it as best you can.

Child Care When You Go Back to Work

There are many reasons why you may find yourself looking for child care for your baby or child with GERD. Financial reasons are often at the forefront; you may have other reasons. Whatever the reason, when you've made the decision, get ready to carry it out as carefully and competently as you have the care giving of your little one. You won't be the first parent of a baby or child with GERD to rely on child care, and you won't be the last.

LETTING GO

The process of going back to work begins with letting go. From going out to dinner with your spouse to returning to employment, leaving your infant or child with reflux in the care of others may seem like the last thing you want to do. You may have feelings of protectiveness. You may think she will only take a bottle if you feed her or a child care provider won't know what to do when she starts shrieking. In other words, no one can replace you in the child care department.

You may feel pressure from others to let go, have some fun or go out on a date with your spouse. But you are just not ready-yet. Be sure to verbalize your fears and concerns to others. Make it clear to your spouse that you would LOVE to carve out some couples time like in your "before reflux" days. Your spouse needs to know that you are not choosing one over the other. It is just that you have to feel comfortable allowing someone else to care for the baby.

> ### *It Does Work:*
>
> I felt like a queen for the day. I spent the morning getting my hair and nails done and then went out to lunch with a friend. I called about a million times to see how they were doing. My husband told me that everything was under control. It has made such a big difference in my life to go out after being isolated so long.

It may take some extra planning and time to let go. Take the time. You may need to start slowly by allowing a family member to care for the baby while you are in another part of the house. Dad, grandma or a family friend may be the obvious choice because they are invested in the baby and know you and your family best. You can show them your caretaking routine carefully constructed from your many hours of trial and error.

But part of letting go is seeing that another person may have their own way of dealing with a situation. Give them a little room to develop their own plan, even when you may know intuitively that your way works better. In the long run, it is best to give everyone a little room to do their own thing. Soon, you may feel comfortable going out of the house for an hour or two. Remember, things may go better or worse than expected. Try to be patient and realize that everyone is doing the best they can.

ACCEPTING YOUR DECISION

The reality is that many mothers delay their return to work until the reflux is under control. Some do this by taking extended leave or leave without pay. Others have no choice but to quit their job if there are no leave options or leave can no longer be extended. Whatever your reason for leaving your job, at some point you will find yourself ready to go back to work.

When that time comes, you may feel guilty that you won't be able to take care of your baby during the day. You may also feel cheated; you have taken care of your baby during the worst of the reflux and now that she is feeling better, someone else will enjoy every smile and playful moment.

You may have a lot of worries about finding day care, particularly whether the new caretaker will be as patient about the crying and vomiting as you. You know how frustrated you get, what about a child care provider? Will she like my baby? What about someone who has to care for many children, not just yours? Will she take care of her like I do and hold her after meals like I instructed her to?

> ## A Day Care Challenge...
>
> Every time he vomited, the day care center called and told me to come and get him. The day care rule was that a child who vomited was "sick" and needed to be separated from the other children. I talked to the director, explaining that he had reflux. But she still had to follow the procedures. Finally, I had the doctor write a note explaining that the vomiting was from reflux.

Like preparing for managing the care of your child with GERD, getting ready to be away everyday, all day takes careful thought and planning. Your goal is to prepare yourself in whatever way you need so you can focus on your new workplace.

FINDING A GOOD MATCH

You will need to spend some time looking at all of the options, deciding what type of care situation you prefer and then selecting a provider. There are many factors going into your decision, not the least of which is cost and availability. Finding a child care provider you feel comfortable with is the key.

Some parents choose in-home care so that their baby gets one-to-one care. In this type of situation, you have more control over how your child is cared for and the schedule.

Some parents choose a group child care situation; it allows your child to be around other children which may help a picky eater experience a positive feeding environment. Find out if special permission is needed for a special feeding schedule or positioning. There are many children in day care with a variety of health issues. Don't hesitate to clearly state the needs of your child and ask the doctor for a note if needed.

From Jan's Blog at www.healthcentral.com:

When Rebecca was a baby, I planned to go back to work. I placed an ad in the newspaper in an effort to hire a babysitter and even interviewed several candidates. But, here is the ad I *really* wanted to place in the Help Wanted section:

CHILD CARE PROVIDER WANTED: Nursing experience or nursing degree preferred. Emergency Medical Technician, CPR instructor or equivalent considered. Lightening quick reflexes and good instincts are a must. Able to administer medication, mix formula, take vital signs and hold a 20 pound baby for 8 hours a day. Willing to perform simple household tasks such as removing vomit stains and odor from the rug and couch. Pay commensurate with experience.

Whatever your choice, by communicating effectively and working together as a team, your child will thrive with someone other than you as a child care provider. It will take education, patience, flexibility and ingenuity not only to make it work, but to make success possible.

THE CARE AND KEEPING OF YOUR DAY CARE PROVIDER

Once you have found a wonderful child care provider, it is important to support her and let her know how important she is to you and your family. Don't forget the frustration and anxiety you feel caring for your child with reflux; empathy is important in caring for your child's new care giver. You know how exhausted you feel after a full day of holding and comforting. Your child care provider must feel the same way. Verbalize these feelings and watch for signs that she is feeling stressed.

If she is providing care in your home, she may be isolated from other adults. In a day care center, the child care providers can give each other a break to eat lunch or care for a less needy child. Let her share her feelings and concerns with you. It is important to keep the lines of communication open so you can both ask questions and resolve problems effectively.

She may have concerns and questions about the reflux, too. Be sure to communicate information from the doctor. You may even want to invite her to a doctor's appointment so she can hear the recommendations directly and report to the doctor what she is seeing from her point of view.

It is vitally important to provide extra support and encouragement to a child care provider who must care for a high-need baby or child all day.

Here are my top tips for the care and keeping of your day care provider when your baby has reflux:

Listen: It is important to be a good listener. When you arrive to pick up your baby, don't rush off. Spend a few moments and really listen. Let her tell you about the day, what happened and find out her concerns.

Let her vent: She might need to vent about the spit up or the marathon crying episode. Let her know that you understand how difficult this is and use the conversation as an opportunity to discuss strategies.

162

Communicate: Be sure to communicate your expectations for her regarding medication, feeding and sleep. Don't forget to tell her what the doctor said at the appointment and the new treatment plan. Give her the expectation that you want to know her questions and concerns.

Written communication: You may want to develop a system of communication such as a notebook or chart to write down observations. Your child care provider needs to know about a rough, sleepless night just as much as you need to know about vomiting episodes during the day. It may be helpful to write down instructions for each task such as feeding, medication, tummy time, etc. Find a quick, easy system such as a checklist.

Nurture: Nurture her and acknowledge her work by complimenting her, saying thank you, and telling her specific examples of her wonderful work. Her experience is full of uncertainty, too, so comments like these go a long way: "I told everyone at work how wonderful you are!" or "I tried your suggestion for feeding her baby food and it worked like a charm." You will make her day!

Presents are nice: Find out a bit about your child care provider and surprise her with a present. If your baby is fussy from getting a new tooth, include a candy bar in the diaper bag with a little note. Remember her birthday and give her a paid day off when needed. If she has children of her own, offer to take care of her children so she can go out to dinner with her spouse. If your budget allows, give her a gift that allows her to pamper herself: restaurant gift card, manicure or massage.

Emergency Plans: Be sure to develop a plan for illnesses and emergencies before an emergency occurs. Make sure she knows how to reach you and the doctor. Let her know that you appreciate hearing from her for any question or concern.

Help for the Helper: In the early weeks, it might help to schedule a helper for the primary care giver. Perhaps you can visit on your lunch hour and spend a few moments feeding your baby or rocking her to sleep. Or you could send Grandma over to visit during the afternoon fussy period or to hold the baby upright after the feeding so your child care provider can take care of the other children or take a brief break.

Your care and concern for your child care provider may help to build a strong foundation for a positive experience for your baby and a long term relationship with a child care provider for your family.

WORRIES ABOUT ABUSE

In rare cases, a child care provider has shaken a baby or in some way caused injury. This is a terrifying thought for all parents. You already know that taking care of your high need baby can be exhausting and may cause feelings of anger. Address this issue directly with your child care provider. Talk about how to handle a situation where she gets to the end of her rope. Should she call you? Should she bring the baby to a neighbor? Should she put the baby in her crib and close the door and then call you? Make it clear that you would be grateful to receive a call for assistance and you would admire her for knowing when she has gotten to the point where she can't go on. Remind her periodically about your concern for her and the plan for this type of situation.

Look on the Bright Side

This chapter has covered all aspects of parenting a baby or child with reflux, issues ranging from common concerns to coping strategies to day care. As difficult as the journey has been, many parents report that dealing with reflux has given them a new outlook at life. Let's listen to some of their perceptions.

I don't take anything for granted.
I take one day at a time.
I don't worry about the little stuff as much.
I have a special bond with my child since we spent so much
  time together.
I can read her like a book.
I have met new friends.

I have received support and help from others and that has
  given me hope.
I have helped her get well.
We have weathered the storm together.

PART 3 ▶ REFLUX IN OLDER CHILDREN

13 ►REFLUX IN OLDER CHILDREN

Many people are surprised to learn that reflux may be just as common in childhood as adulthood or infancy. Estimates are that millions of older children are diagnosed or continue to suffer with Gastroesophageal Reflux Disease, yet their illness is overshadowed by the growing awareness of GER in infancy and by the pharmaceutical companies' advertising for adult GERD.

Symptoms, diagnosis and treatment of older children have many similarities to those of infants with GERD. Reading earlier chapters on GER and GERD will provide detailed information about the topics presented in this chapter. However, there are significant differences. In this chapter, we will focus on some of the special situations an older child with GER/GERD may experience, such as going to school, participating in sports and eating.

Characteristics of GER and GERD in Older Children

GER IN OLDER CHILDREN

Experiencing the normal physiological process of gastroesophageal reflux (GER) is not uncommon in older children. Diagnosing an older child with GER is different from a baby in one important sense: your older child can describe symptoms and can grasp some of what you say about the diagnosis and treatment process. A pattern of reflux symptoms may develop gradually, getting more noticeable and prompting a visit to the doctor for a diagnosis of reflux. Symptoms may include regurgitation or backwashing of stomach contents into the esophagus or throat, burping, an occasional bad taste in the mouth, or stomachache. These symptoms are often associated with eating a large meal, eating in a hurry, engaging in physical activity after a meal, or stress.

GER is not a disease and does not require medical treatment. Parents often find that monitoring diet, sleep and activities helps to identify triggers for the symptoms. Implementing some lifestyle changes can go a long way toward home management of GER symptoms, such as limiting fast food, making time for eating slowly and looking to minimize stress.

GERD IN OLDER CHILDREN

For some families, GERD in childhood is a continuation of reflux diagnosed in infancy. Your screaming spitter became the world's pickiest eater at age two. Then, instead of your child

---

From the Experience of a GERD Mom...

I have 4 active boys who regularly eat me out of house and home. However, my 8 year old is the picky eater of the family. He is the one who comes home with a stomachache after a baseball game or a day at the amusement park while the other boys seem just fine. When the stomach flu hit the household, he always gets the worst case and it lasts longer than the other kids. Recently, he was diagnosed with acid reflux by his pediatrician and now takes medication as needed.

◆

We thought our daughter's reflux was long gone but when she was three she started to have wet burps after meals. Within a few months, she had lost weight too.

---

outgrowing GERD, you find yourself explaining details of your child's digestive system to her teacher. You are continuing the routine of exploring treatment options, following the well worn path between doctors and pharmacists. Only now there is a difference—your child is out in the world, and instead of the daily struggle to get your child to eat, you are discussing and negotiating what can and cannot be eaten at her best friend's birthday party.

While it is common for babies with reflux to spit up or vomit, older children with GERD tend to have slightly different symptoms. Often they experience silent reflux (the sensation of food coming up the esophagus) or heartburn, or they may have a stomachache. A pattern of frequent symptoms that interfere with quality of life, including eating, sleeping, school work and behavior, are the basis for a diagnosis of GERD. Health consequences, affecting breathing and growth, and other complications are more likely to occur in older children with GERD.

Below are the more common symptoms. Your child may experience one or two consistently or there may be a combination of symptoms.

Pain: Chest pain, also known as heartburn, is a common characteristic of childhood GERD. Some children report a sore throat and discomfort in their stomach, above the belly button, in their back or shoulders.

Discomfort during and after eating: Silent reflux or the sensation of food coming up the esophagus and throat is common. Your child may experience wet/sour burps, loud belches or wet hiccups after a meal. Some children report that it feels like food is stuck in the throat. Nausea and vomiting are rare symptoms in older children, but may occur.

Picky Eating: Some children with GERD learn through trial and error to avoid certain foods that trigger reflux symptoms (such as orange juice and tomatoes). GERD can also lead to extremely picky eating or an eating disorder if the diet is limited to a few foods or entire food groups are avoided by your child.

Growth Issues: Sometimes a sudden weight loss is a sign that a child has GERD. Other children may have a pattern of slow weight gain due to picky eating. It is also possible for a child with GERD to be overweight from frequent eating and drinking to rinse out their mouth and push the acid back down.

Sleep: GERD can contribute to restless sleep and frequent night waking. Nocturnal reflux occurs when the reclined position causes backwashing of acid, coughing or choking. A poor sleep pattern may lead to chronic fatigue and poor functioning during the day. Apnea and obstructive sleep disorders are rare.

Behavior: If a child with GERD experiences chronic pain and discomfort, behavioral problems such as tantrums may be seen. Over time, there may be anxiety, depression, or poor attention.

Respiratory: Children with GERD may experience a hoarse or deep sounding voice, throat clearing and a cough from acid exposure to the throat and esophagus. Doctors believe that some children may have more frequent respiratory infections or ear and sinus infections. Acid may irritate the lungs and cause wheezing, asthma, and, in rare cases, *laryngospasm* (a severe type of choking episode).

Dental: Repeated acid exposure to the teeth may cause some children to have an increase in tooth enamel erosion and cavities. Some parents and dentists report bad breath, and excessive saliva production.

Esophagus: The delicate surface of the esophagus is not designed for repeated acid exposure. Untreated GERD may lead to esophagitis (redness and swelling) and, in rare instances, esophageal ulcers and strictures (narrowing of the esophagus). While Barrett's Esophagus (a pre-cancerous condition) is a concern for adults with GERD, it is a rare complication of GERD in children.

COMPLICATIONS

Older children may experience long term acid exposure leading to irritation of the wall of the esophagus and stomach. When the acid exposure progresses to the point of irritation or damage, a doctor will use the term *esophagitis*. Most children respond positively to an array of treatments and manage their GERD with minimal modifications to their lifestyle. However, for a few children treatment is less conclusive. They continue to have symptoms or exhibit unusual symptoms needing further

treatment or surgery (Section 4, Advanced Medical Topics, offers details, should you require them).

BEHAVIOR AND CHRONIC PAIN/ILLNESS

A child in chronic pain may exhibit a wide range of behaviors from being withdrawn to overly active, upset or

agitated. Your child may need a different kind of parenting to deal with the special circumstances of her chronic health condition. Sometimes you have to bend the rules a little if your child isn't feeling well. If it seems like the "well" periods are quite short with very little time when things are normal, you may need to be exceptionally creative in your approach.

All children like rules and routines, so having a schedule and a predictable sequence to the day makes everyone feel more in control. Often, school provides this type of secure, predictable routine as well. If your child is missing school often due to illness, she may feel out of step with her friends. If chronic pain is affecting her school performance or behavior at home, talk to the doctor about treatment to manage pain.

If your child is chronically ill, she may have developed some fears and phobias about doctors and medical care.

Crying, resisting treatment and temper tantrums may be her way of expressing fear and distress. You may need to work with the medical staff to help her verbalize her concerns and to work through behavioral issues. If the problems persist, seek counseling for her.

Older Kids: Diagnosis and Treatment

It is a bit easier to diagnose a child than a baby; they can verbalize their symptoms and concerns to you and to the doctor. Even a very young child should be encouraged to tell the doctor where it hurts and what foods taste yucky.

Sometimes parents and children have special code names for reflux. One little girl would tell her mom she had "yucky stuff" in her mouth. Another child would tell her mother, "I have a crumb in my throat." Since many children don't have a good concept of time, this type of communication helps you to track the symptoms and document the frequency of the problem.

The process of diagnosis and treatment is the same with older children as it is with infants (Chapter 9, "The Reflux Roller Coaster: From Diagnosis to Treatment"). You will need your carefully documented notes to answer the doctors many questions. She will look at your child's rate of growth and then conduct an exam before making a diagnosis of reflux.

Age appropriate opportunities for your child in the diagnosis of "what's wrong" may start a pattern of involvement that is helpful in the treatment of this chronic disease. Keeping your child involved in the process may help as your active child learns to manage her GERD in the months or years to come. Treatment may also include managing other causes of digestive discomfort such as constipation, lactose intolerance and food allergies (Chapter 9 provides a full description of the common treatments).

As with infants, older children will have the same process of *Empiric Diagnosis*: trying a treatment to confirm a diagnosis. You will follow the same routine of home treatment, perhaps medication—perhaps several medications one right after the

Does she really have a stomachache?

It can be confusing for parents, doctors and the school nurse to determine if a stomachache is related to GERD or another cause. We all know that a large number of children show up at the nurses office on Monday morning with a "really bad" stomachache. School avoidance, stress at home or school and other problems can lead to a visit to the nurse.

We all know that our stomach does respond to stress at times. It is likely your stomach will churn while waiting for the big job interview or before you make the big presentation to the committee. It is important to talk with your child, the school nurse, the teacher and the doctor about the pattern of symptoms you are seeing. Perhaps your child has a nervous stomach. On the other hand, your child may have GERD and her stomach is the first part of her body to respond to stress and illness. If the symptoms are not clear, a doctor may suggest having your child evaluated by a mental health professional. This can seem really harsh to a child and a parent. It is not uncommon for a counselor to wear two hats and make a medical diagnosis: her head is just fine but her stomach really hurts!

other. Your documentation and note taking will be equally important. Your advantage is that you and your child can work together to describe the symptoms and assess treatment.

HOME TREATMENT AND LIFESTYLE CHOICES

In Chapters 4, 5 and 9 we discuss the various home treatment options that are prescribed for infants. Older children benefit from many of the same treatments prescribed for young children. These include: lifestyle modification, medication, and a special diet. See Part 2, Gastroesophageal Reflux Disease (GERD) for a full description of the treatments available. However, there are some differences for older children and here are a few.

Positioning: If your child wakes up at night or seems tired after a full night in bed, it might help to elevate the head of the bed. You may have to try several strategies to get your child comfortably elevated.

Extra Pillows: **Some children do fine with an extra pillow or two. A wedge pillow is preferable because it elevates the whole torso and avoids bending the stomach.**

Bed Blocks: **Try using bed blocks under the head of the bed. They are available at most bedding stores. The blocks may be stacked to gain extra height.**

Wedge: **A commercially made wedge can be placed on a bed to elevate the head and upper body. The resource section contains information on commercially made wedges for all ages from newborn to teens.**

Recliner Chair: **Some children feel comfortable sleeping in a recliner chair.**

Healthy lifestyle: It's not just about feeding any more. When your child was little, you had complete control over her environment. Now that she spends some time away from your house, she will be making her own decisions, especially as she approaches the teen years.

Be sure to tell her that it is important to avoid alcohol and tobacco; they are certain to aggravate reflux. There is some evidence that GERD may be linked to exposure to tobacco smoke.

It is likely that a typical childhood diet of frequent fast food meals, carbonated beverages and caffeine may cause a worsening of GERD in children.

Maintaining a healthy weight or losing weight through healthy eating and exercise will go a long way toward managing GERD. There is some evidence that obesity may be linked to GERD.

Loose clothing: Your older child may be very invested in wearing certain clothes based on the latest fashion trends.

Hopefully, the "style of the week" will include wearing loosely fitting clothes around the waist. Tights, tight fitting jeans and pants may put more pressure on the stomach, especially after a meal and cause pain and bloating.

MEDICATION

In Chapter 11, "Medications for Reflux," you will find general information on giving medication. For details on specific medications, Chapter 15 provides introductory details on a wide range of those commonly prescribed.

Older children, especially those treated for GERD from infancy, may have developed some opinions and attitudes about medication. All children are different; some like a particular flavor of liquid medication, while others like dissolving medicine or prefer a pill to swallow quickly without any taste. Not all medications offer these options, but it is important to try to make the medicine as appealing as possible (see flavoring and compounding in Chapter 11). Let your doctor know what works best for your child. The goal is to be sure the medication is taken everyday, and if it is tolerable your child will be much more likely to meet that goal.

Give your child a simple explanation about why she needs the medication and help her to communicate any side effects and symptoms to you and the doctor. If your child seems reluctant to take medication, try to determine why. Sometimes kids refuse to take medication because it tastes bad or burns the throat. Other children need some kind of incentive like a happy face chart or other reward system to increase success.

An older child may want to assist in measuring and preparing medication as a way to feel in control. In most cases, it is a good idea to foster independence and good self care habits. If your child takes some control over administering medications, remind her that a parent must always be present during medication time. It may be confusing for a child to differentiate between candy and a fruit flavored, pink, and chewy over the counter medication.

It appears that some children with reflux have a higher rate of tooth enamel erosion. More research is needed to determine how common this problem is and how to prevent it. Meanwhile, children with reflux need to be monitored closely by the dentist from the moment the first tooth erupts. You will receive instructions on careful brushing and other treatments to protect the teeth. It is a good idea to encourage your child to rinse out her mouth with water following a reflux episode.

> ### *A Reflux Mom Says...*
>
> Even though I am so careful to help with tooth brushing, my four year old with reflux has one or more cavities at each check up. My eleven year old (without reflux) still has not had one cavity her entire life

Your child may complain that the toothpaste tastes bad or causes backwashing. Try experimenting with other brands or try toothpaste for sensitive teeth. Brushing with water is not as effective as using toothpaste, but it is better than not brushing.

A child with oral hypersensitivity or a strong gag reflex may resist tooth brushing completely. You may need to monitor tooth brushing and work with the dentist or a speech language pathologist to help your child accept brushing.

Your Child with GERD Goes to School

BEING OUT IN THE WORLD

Perhaps the most significant difference between a baby or toddler with reflux and a preschooler or older child is that they are not spending the majority of their waking hours at home. If you went back to work, you may have found it difficult to surrender control of your child's care to a care taker.

Now, you're facing letting go again (Chapter 9, High Need Parenting). Only this time, the environment is more complex and the array of care givers has increased while your control has decreased. Nevertheless, you continue to be your child's advocate and you are an expert on GERD. Education, explanation, and encouragement are your advocacy tools of choice. Sometimes stronger measures may be called for and you will need to use them…with sometimes as many as five people in one school!

GOING TO PRESCHOOL

It may be hard to let your little one go to preschool. You both have been through so much together. You may have concerns about all the "what ifs": What if she needs me? What if she doesn't feel well? What if she cries for me? Take your time and do things in small steps when necessary. Let the preschool staff know where to find you in an emergency and about the special care she needs (diet, medication, extra snacks).

Your child will look to you for cues about how to behave. It is important for you to give her permission and confidence as she steps forward toward independence. You are still the most precious person in the world to her perhaps in a deeper sense. Your relationship may be even more special since you have been on such an important journey together. She will always remember your special closeness and return to tell you all about her adventures in the big world.

BEYOND PRESCHOOL

Your child may need to eat a special diet or eat frequent small meals to manage her reflux while at school, just like at home. It may be necessary to meet with the school nurse and teacher to develop a plan for the classroom. School schedules and policies may get in the way of good eating to manage reflux. It isn't always easy to convince the school staff about the importance of following a treatment plan. Your child may look as healthy as the other kids in the class so it may not seem that medical treatment is needed.

Eating those snacks or small meals in the classroom may be hard for your child, as well as her teacher. Your child may get a great deal of attention for being allowed to eat in the classroom. Other children may ask why they can't eat "but she can." Working with your child's teacher so she has clear and ready answers can make a big difference in your child's willingness to eat as she should.

Jan says:

My daughter had a hard time eating lunch with her class since it was the last lunch period of the day. If she didn't eat a snack in the late morning when the hunger pains started she would have a stomachache. By the time her lunch period would come, she was so hungry that she inhaled her food and ingested a lot of air. This caused bloating and pain that lasted the rest of the afternoon. We had to make sure she had a snack or the day was a total loss.

◆

My daughter was really self conscious about eating her snack at her desk. Day after day, she told me that she wasn't really hungry and didn't need a snack. I started giving her snacks that she could eat without being noticed—forget the noisy wrapper or crunchy food. She kept a baggie of breakfast cereal or bite sized crackers on her lap and took out one piece at a time when no one was looking.

Sometimes a school nurse or teacher will believe that a stomachache is a sign that a child is trying to avoid school or has an emotional problem. It may be necessary for the pediatric gastroenterologist to write a letter to the school describing the situation and the treatment that is needed during the school day.

Jan says:

The doctor wrote a note on his prescription pad for the school. The note stated that my daughter was to have drinks and snacks at her desk throughout the day.

If your child coughs, belches or burps after a meal, this can be very distracting and cause a burping contest in a matter of seconds. All of this unwanted attention can cause your child a great deal of embarrassment. Some children explain that they have reflux while others simply say, "My reflux makes me burp really loud." Be sure to talk to your child about school and develop a plan together. Check in periodically and make sure everything is going smoothly. It is also important to check in with the school staff and thank them for helping your child.

JAN'S LESSONS LEARNED[2]

Going to school with reflux has taught me so many lessons about managing reflux during the school day, whether it is preschool or elementary school. As parents, we have developed a fine tuned plan for managing reflux at home and it may be stressful to turn over control of the plan to the school team. The reality is you and your child will have some challenges and extra work. But in the end, your child will be successful at learning new skills including some lessons that may not be in the curriculum.

Lesson #1: Reflux is more common than you might think.

Even though reflux is a common medical condition of childhood, you may not know any other children with reflux. You may feel a bit isolated, as if your child has some rare problem. I remember volunteering in my daughter's science class and coincidentally the lesson was on the digestive system. During the class, the teacher mentioned that she and her son both had gastroesophageal reflux. A hand shot up in the air and another student indicated that she had reflux, too. My daughter and I looked at each other with a mixture of surprise and amusement. We were both convinced that she was the only kid in the entire school with gastroesophageal reflux and here was a child she had known for several years yet we had no idea she had reflux too. It is likely there are other children with reflux at school, attending daycare or taking piano lessons and you didn't even know it.

Lesson #2: Your child may be self-conscious about reflux.

---

[2] These lessons were developed in Jan's Blog at www.healthcentral.com.

What kid wants to stand out at school? Most children want to blend in by wearing the right clothes and carrying the newest backpack. Sometimes even the contents of the lunch bag needs to conform to the coolness rules. Managing all of this may be challenging if your child is on a special diet or needs special accommodations at school such as extra meal breaks or trips to the nurse for medication. It is likely your child will be faced with questions from curious classmates too. The end result is that many children will try to hide their reflux and try to blend in with the crowd.

Lesson # 3: Your child may do better than you think at school.

You may worry about sending your child with reflux to school. It may seem that she will do poorly without your care or the school staff will not attend to her needs like you do. The reality is most children with reflux do just fine in school. They adapt to new routines, meet new friends and have enriching experiences.

Lesson #4: Your child can participate in sports.

With the proper medical treatment and diet, your child should be able to participate in most sports. Some children find that certain sports such as wrestling and gymnastics put too much pressure on abdominal muscles, leading to increased reflux episodes. Trial and error is still the best way to figure out what works!

Careful eating and medication are, as always, a good way to help your child play the sports she wants while still keeping the reflux under control. Your child may respond well to a change in diet (light eating before exercise) or well-timed medication (such as before a sporting event). Consult your child's physician or a sports medicine specialist for advice.

14 ▶ FEEDING YOUR PRESCHOOLER AND OLDER CHILD

You, like most parents of a child with reflux, may face many challenges while getting your child to eat, much less eat what is healthy! You worry about nutrition and calories as well as hidden ingredients listed in fine print on the label. Your child may have settled on a small selection of foods that she will eat...no substitutions! The doctor or dietician may have given you a list of foods to eat and foods to avoid. Well meaning friends and relatives offer helpful hints and advice about feeding and nutrition. In the end, all the information, advice and admonishments leave you with is conflicting information.

All this can be very wearing on a worried mom or dad— and very normal for parents whose child has reflux. Within a few months, feeding your child may have left you feeling frustrated and defeated about the whole process. Maybe you dread each meal; you can't think of what to feed your child because nothing seems to work. Out of all this desperation you may find you suffer from "waitress syndrome," spending hours in the kitchen cooking special meals your child won't touch, much less try! You find yourself angry at your child, even forcing her to eat. You know this isn't the answer, but you just don't know what to do.

What ever you do, feeding remains at the center of treatment for your child's GERD (Gastroesophageal Reflux Disease).

Feeding Patterns in the Older Child

Feeding your older child is not like feeding an infant. You may face new challenges and new road blocks in your efforts to see your child eat and grow. Not the least of which is your fear of having your child leave, the safe, routine environment you've created.

Here's a "portrait" of the parent of an older child with reflux. Maybe you will recognize yourself!

Your child's food list contains a handful of items such as apple juice, crackers and chicken nuggets.

Your child strictly adheres to the "White Diet" or "Prison Diet": rice, mashed potatoes, chicken and saltines.

You worry about food intake all of the time. You even keep a food diary.

You show signs of waitress syndrome; you cook special meals for your child, spending hours in the kitchen.

You follow your child around the house with a bowl of food or a sippy cup all day long, trying to feed a sip here, a bit there.

Your purse, diaper bag and mini van all contain a food pantry stocked with snack foods and drinks.

You call Grandma when your child eats 3 bites of food in a meal.

You feel angry and defeated about feeding your child.

You can't even tell when your child is hungry; her signals are very confusing.

It seems like you work much too hard to get your child to eat compared to others.

Whether this list reflects some part or all of you life, it helps to know why your child won't—or can't—eat like she should. Here are a few reasons. When you think about it, they are pretty reasonable reasons! But, still…she has to eat!

CAREFUL EATER…PICKY EATER

A child may be labeled a picky eater if she eats a small variety of foods, eats a small quantity of food or is a food grazer—eating a bit here, a nibble there, all day long.

Actually, it might be more accurate to call her a "careful eater"; she knows from painful experience that each food item she puts in her mouth could leave a bad taste or trigger a reflux episode. Foods can also trigger pain, burping, bloating, stomach or chest pain or a burning sensation in the throat. Older children report that they can taste the food they ate an hour ago or taste vomit in their mouth when the food and stomach contents back wash. Bending over or engaging in vigorous activity after a meal can trigger symptoms. Wouldn't you be a "picky eater" if you tasted vomit and acid in your mouth after every meal?!

> ### Jan says:
>
> I believe it is unfair to call a child with reflux a picky eater. I like to say she is a "careful eater." Just as someone who is allergic to peanuts is careful, even vigilant, about avoiding peanuts at all costs, a child with reflux is careful about avoiding foods that trigger a reflux episode.

All this can make feeding a preschooler or older child with reflux very time consuming and very difficult. It is easy to blame yourself for feeding problems. But remember, it takes two to tango. You and your child need to interact and work together to make feeding successful. It is your job to provide healthy foods at appropriate intervals and it is the job of your child to eat familiar foods, try new foods and acquire new feeding skills. If she doesn't seem to be able to do her part of the job, you need to find out why rather than blame yourself.

> ### A GERD Mom Says...
>
> One of the hardest things for me is when others don't understand that my child struggles with eating. It is so stressful to hear the comments. If I had a dollar for everybody who suggested I try chocolate because all kids like it, I would be rich.

CARBOHYDRATE CRAVING

Your child may prefer what is affectionately called the "White Diet" or "Prison Diet." She will only eat plain, white food such as rice, mashed potatoes and chicken. It is thought that a high carbohydrate diet is easier to digest and that some kids crave carbohydrates. These foods are considered "comfort food" for kids with reflux.

NOT HUNGRY

Your child may not have clear hunger signals, so it is hard to know when to feed her. Her stomach may not understand the concept of breakfast, lunch and dinner. This means she is likely to nibble all day and hardly feel full or hungry.

HAVING AN "EATING WINDOW"

An "eating window" is a time of day when eating is less painful and most calories are consumed. This could be anywhere from mid-morning to late afternoon. If your child is in school during this important eating opportunity, it is vital to make arrangements with the school for healthy eating at this time.

FEEDING AVERSION

A child may be labeled as having a feeding disorder or feeding aversion if careful eating escalates to an extreme level.

It may be time to speak to your child's physician about her extremely selective habits if: you can count the number of

186

foods your child eats on one hand; whole food groups are missing from your child's diet; or your child seems afraid to eat. It may be necessary to consult with a feeding specialist or a feeding team to manage your child's discomfort from eating and to decrease behavioral patterns that developed as a result of the pain of eating.

Top Tips from Reflux Moms' Kitchens

Nothing is more frustrating for a mom or dad than to be constantly focused on what your child with reflux is eating or won't eat or can't eat...and on and on. Trial and error is the watchword for Reflux Moms. Many of the strategies listed here and developed below have helped parents improve the eating experience for their child...and peace of mind for you!

Offer small, frequent meals.
Establish a routine.
Play with your food.
Check your emotions at the kitchen door.
Quiet play following a meal.
Reflux diet.
Nutritional drinks and vitamins.
Identify sensory and oral motor issues.
Identify food allergies and intolerances.
Manage pain.
Celebrate special occasions.

187

SMALL, FREQUENT MEALS

A child may benefit from small, frequent meals rather than the traditional breakfast, lunch and dinner. It might make sense to split a healthy meal into two parts. For instance, eat half of a sandwich at one meal and the other half a few hours later. Some children find it is better to avoid beverages with meals and only drink liquids between meals.

ESTABLISH A ROUTINE

Nothing has been the same since the birth of your child. Remember how you used to sit at the table and eat a meal with real dishes and even forks?! While eating a family meal may have gone by the wayside, now is the time to revive that lost pleasure and establish a family meal routine.

A GERD Mom Says...

I thought the reflux was getting better because she stopped vomiting at 6 months of age. Then I realized her symptoms had changed and now she had silent reflux.

It is probably not realistic to have each and every meal together as a family. Try to focus on one meal a day when most family members are together and there is more time. Sitting at the table together, TV and radio off and no one plugged into their iPod, is an essential part of teaching your child how to eat with others. Parents are watched closely by little eyes, passing on eating habits and attitudes to their children. You set the tone by engaging in pleasant conversation, eating slowly, and

---

Jan Says...

Instead of saying, "Snack Time" (which implies cookies and sugary juice); I named the snacks for the foods we would eat. In the morning, we always had our "Fruit Snack" and in the afternoon we always had our "Yogurt Snack." After they had consumed the main snack food, they could nibble on other foods such as crackers.

◆

Dr. Bill Sears, author of *The Baby Book*, tells his patients with reflux, "Eat half as much and twice as often and remember to chew twice as long."

---

following a simple routine. Let your child see you trying new foods and eating all of those fruits and vegetables we know they are trying to avoid. Also, consider your child's age and limit mealtime to a time based on your child's age and developmental level.

Perhaps it is like a three ring circus in your house at mealtime; someone spills the glass of milk while someone else complains about the menu and the phone rings as you are answering the door. It may take time to establish a routine. Take it slowly. Every meal will not be perfect.

CHECK YOUR EMOTIONS AT THE KITCHEN DOOR

Feeding may have been an unpleasant experience from day one, not only for your child but for you as well. You may feel tremendous pressure to help your child gain weight, eat nutritious foods, and catch up on feeding milestones. It doesn't help that others blame you for holding your child back or even say you have caused her feeding issues. It is easy to put pressure on your child, hoping she will rise to the occasion. Usually, just the opposite occurs: you put the pressure on; she feels cornered and refuses to eat with even greater will and noisy crying.

189

Somehow your anger and frustration about eating (or more likely the lack of eating) needs to be left at the kitchen door.

A GERD Mom Says...

She is doing well now, but the road has been tough. My daughter went through many stages where she refused to eat. The biggest challenge was when she would chew her food, then spit it out because she knew that eating hurt her throat. She would try to avoid swallowing even though she was clearly hungry.

◆

The doctor told me to stop worrying about what and how often she eats. He said kids will eat when they get hungry enough, if we leave them alone (keep in mind that this was advice for a child in a healthy weight range). Because I was desperate, I tried it. To my amazement, it worked. When it wasn't a battle anymore, she started to eat. It wasn't perfect but I decided this was going to have to be okay.

This can be hard if a "meal" consists of 5 Cheerios and a few sips of milk. Or when your specially cooked meal is soundly rejected by a very harsh food critic: your little one sitting in a chair with a stern look on her face.

Sometimes you will find yourself unable to face the feeding challenges. If this happens, ask someone else to help with mealtime. Perhaps dad can take charge of a meal and you leave the room or even leave the house.

Sometimes control over eating is a big issue. Older kids want to assert their independence by making food choices and deciding when and where they will eat. You may come across as the "healthy food police" and the kitchen may become a battleground. Older children need to learn to self select foods that do not cause

Jan says:

I was surprised when my 11 year old told me she didn't think she should drink soda anymore. I think it was embarrassing to burp really loud and it was making her reflux worse. I asked her what she wanted to drink instead and made a mental note to buy a lot!

190

digestive issues. This is your challenge: just as you help your older child achieve independence in other situations, you want to help her become skilled at listening to her stomach and remembering to use self control and healthy habits.

Advice from a professional...

Consciously decide to focus on the emotions of gratitude at each meal. Choose at least one aspect of the meal that you appreciate. Tell yourself how much you are thankful for the part of the meal. As you become more comfortable with a focus on gratitude, observe your child at the meal and share something that you appreciate about your child. Select something about her approach to the meal, such as "I loved the way you decided to find out about the carrots" or "I really enjoyed listening to your story about the school lunchroom. It felt like being there."

Suzanne Evans Morris, Ph.D., founder and director, New Visions

---

PLAY WITH YOUR FOOD

While you are establishing your mealtime routine, remember to have a little fun. Eating may feel like serious work to both you and your child. Try to keep things light and humorous. Take a look at mealtime from your child's point of view and make sure eating is pleasurable.

Young children love to feed mom or dad. Let your child give you all of the broccoli trees and apple slices she won't touch. Be sure to emphasize how delicious the food is and thank her over and over again for giving you this delicious food. She will think this is very funny!

Some children thrive on pretend play activities with an eating theme, so get out the miniature tea set and feed the teddy bear, doll and all of the neighborhood children. A change of scenery can help too. Have a picnic at the park or in your play room; eat on a rock or on the jungle gym. Some children respond well to eating with a friend or relative or with other children. A trip out to a restaurant can be very entertaining and distracting during mealtime.

191

Some young children like having a special plate, cup and utensils featuring their favorite character such as Mickey

Jan Says...

Rebecca had many unusual eating patterns. She only wanted to nurse and she refused all baby food and eventually just transitioned to table foods that she could pick up and eat herself. At the same time, she needed to have LOTS of bad tasting medicine by mouth. I had to wrestle her to the ground to get the stuff in. It tasted bad and probably hurt her throat too. She was the perfect candidate for a major feeding aversion/feeding disorder.

However, I used my mommy instincts to make eating a fun, positive, rewarding activity. It took years and years and a lot of patience to let her set the pace. We had our ups and downs but now she is eating normally.

Mouse or Dora the Explorer. Using special plates and cups conveys the message that mealtime is special and yet predictable. Some children feel more secure knowing they can count on the same utensils. Don't worry if you find yourself packing these items for all outings.

Older children should go food shopping with you and help select a new food now and then. Perhaps they have seen another child eating a food or had a new food while a guest at a friend's house. Use a shopping trip to hunt for different types of food. Have your child chose one vegetable, one fruit, one meat. You never know what food or eating experience will stimulate a positive association.

Jan says:

My child became the salad maker of the house. She ripped the lettuce, selected the vegetables and toppings and proudly presented the bowl at the table. Of course she never did eat any of it!

With younger children, reading story books about eating can be very motivating and instructive. Popular books include: *The Very Hungry Caterpillar, Green Eggs and Ham* and *If You Give a Mouse a Cookie.* Use the repetitive nature of these books to playfully talk about eating. In *Green Eggs and Ham*, Sam says, "I

192

do not like green eggs and ham." You can say, "I do not like green eggs and ham...but I do like ham sandwiches. I wonder if Sam would like a ham sandwich just like this one." Older children may be interested in helping with simple food preparation. It doesn't matter if they eat the food or not; it gave them the opportunity to touch and smell the food up close.

QUIET PLAY FOLLOWING A MEAL

Once you release your child from the table, she may resume her usual activities: jumping on the couch, chasing the dog and using the ottoman to practice her football tackling moves. It is best to encourage quiet play (story time, puzzle, art activity) rather than vigorous play. Some children also benefit from scheduling meals at least an hour before bed time so their stomachs are empty when they lay down. At school, older children normally have a snack or lunch followed by recess or free play. While it is fine for most children, children with reflux may develop significant pain from engaging in physical activities right after a meal.

Jan says:

I am not sure there is a diet or food list that would be universal for each child. I think guiding "gerdlings" to positive eating is 50% attitude and 50% careful eating. My daughter was always open to new eating experiences. We did the tea party stage: play with food, eating not mandatory but encouraged. We did the Asian thing: chopsticks and pretty little bowls and accessories. She found that she loved Chinese take out! We tried every bagel at the neighborhood bagel store (a destination via bike) and she settled on spinach bagels as the hands down favorite. Do you see a pattern here?!

A recommended diet? Not really! Through positive associations, playfulness and pure luck, we found some foods that she could tolerate and that fit into our eating patterns. Yes, we still have stacks of frozen macaroni and cheese in the freezer but we also have some foods that our whole family can live with. It is a continuing journey. We gain some new foods and lose some old ones. Illness or a bad reflux day can be enough to take a food off the "safe" list. It can be very frustrating.

REFLUX DIET

Parents always want to know if there is a special diet to manage reflux. Unfortunately, there is not a recommended diet or cookbook just for children. Many children with reflux naturally find that a high carbohydrate diet reduces discomfort. This is affectionately called the White Diet or Prison Diet by many. Children find that carbohydrates such as crackers, pasta, cereal, potatoes and rice are easily digested. These foods are digested quickly and converted to energy.

While many children consume adequate calories on a high carbohydrate diet, there is some concern that the White Diet lacks key nutrients because meat, dairy, fruits and vegetables are largely absent.

Instead of...	Try...
Whole milk, cream	Low fat milk, yogurt
Donuts, cake, cookies	Crackers, pretzels, bread, pasta, rice
Fried chicken, hot dogs, sausage, bacon	Lean beef, chicken
High fat sandwich meat (bologna, salami)	Low fat sandwich meat (oven roasted chicken)
Orange juice, citrus juice, soda, coffee, tea	Water
Oranges, lemon, pineapples	Pears, apple, banana
Beans, cabbage, broccoli, onion	Potatoes, sweet potato, carrots
Spicy food, garlic, peppermint	Light or no spices. Herbs.

The general rule is that children with reflux should eat the foods they can tolerate. Many children find that eating spicy foods and high acid foods (citrus, tomato, pickles, and vinegar) can trigger reflux symptoms. Some foods such as beans and broccoli may cause gas and bloating. High fat foods (fried food, pastry) may trigger symptoms because fats digest slowly and may cause discomfort. However, foods and food groups should not be restricted unless there is a true allergy or a doctor recommends it.

The food list should be used as a general guide for food selection. If a particular food or food group causes discomfort, try an alternate food.

Your older child is bound to push her luck with forbidden foods at friends' houses or at school. It is natural for a child to experiment and try to eat the foods other kids love. They will learn their limits through experience.

DEALING WITH FOOD ALLERGIES AND INTOLERANCES

While adhering to a special diet may be a vital treatment, it can be frustrating to you and your child. Your child may not appreciate your attempts to monitor the foods she eats at home, school and elsewhere. It can be embarrassing to be different, including eating special food.

Well meaning adults and other children may not realize how important it is to adhere to a special diet and may try to offer a child "just a bite." This can have serious health consequences if a serious or life threatening allergic reaction occurs. Your job as a parent is to educate all of the people your child interfaces with and provide alternative foods. Needless to say, many parents feel a great deal of stress about all of the meal planning, shopping, label reading and supervision that goes into that job.

Jan says:

We tried every chewable, gummy, bubble gum vitamin on the shelf and they all caused my daughter to urp and burp. She complained that she could taste the vitamin in her mouth and refused to take them. I think she was refluxing the vitamins. We finally stopped trying a chewable vitamin and switched to a pill she could swallow. Now she doesn't complain about taking the vitamins.

NUTRITIONAL DRINKS, VITAMINS AND MINERAL SUPPLEMENTS

The doctor may keep a toddler on an infant formula beyond age one year and then introduce a nutritional drink for children ages 1-12 years. A vitamin/mineral supplement may be used if there are nutritional deficits from a limited diet.

IDENTIFY ORAL-MOTOR AND SENSORY ISSUES

If a child receives aggressive medical treatment for reflux but still seems afraid to eat or coughs and chokes when eating, an oral-motor or sensory problem may be interfering with eating. A speech language pathologist or occupational therapist can evaluate your child and identify the cause of the feeding problem. Some hospitals and clinics have a feeding team to evaluate and treat feeding issues.

It may take months of feeding therapy to help your child overcome feeding and oral-motor problems. Feeding therapy can be very intense but very helpful. You may be asked to practice exercises and activities at home and come to a clinic weekly or monthly.

MANAGE PAIN

It is important to manage reflux symptoms and pain through diet and medication. A child will have a great deal of anxiety about eating if each bite leads to pain and discomfort. Some children experience pain if they are too hungry, so they nibble and graze; it leaves a bit of food churning in their stomach all day.

Tips for Eating at School[3]

Here are my best tips for helping your refluxer eat at school:

---

3 These tips were developed in Jan's Blog at www.healthcentral.com.

Tip #1: Reflux Diet

I opened the Sunday newspaper last week and saw an article about healthy and fun lunch ideas. It sure didn't look like anything a child with reflux I know would eat! As a reflux mom, I have learned to smile and ignore these articles.

While there isn't a "reflux diet", there are several types of foods that trigger reflux symptoms in many children such as acidic foods (tomato, oranges, and orange juice), high fat foods, spicy foods, carbonated beverages, chocolate and caffeine.

When you're thinking of what to pack for school, try these lunch foods instead:

A baggie of deli meat, breakfast cereal and crackers may provide similar calories and nutrients to a sandwich.
Substitute lactose free nutrition drink or lactose free milk for regular milk.
Offer 100% juice or water rather than sugary drinks.
Substitute yogurt for a high fat pudding cup.
Give the carbohydrate junkies their fill of pretzels, popcorn, crackers, breakfast cereal and granola bars.
Add protein from peanuts and peanut butter (if no peanut allergies).
Make or buy trail mix with peanuts, soy nuts, raisins, etc
Add calcium and protein with drinkable yogurt, cheese sticks and yogurt cups.
Include some veggies and fruit with dip.
Throw in that Hershey kiss if you child tolerates it.
You can attach a small note that says: I love you!

Tip #2: Think Outside the Box

Think outside the box, the lunch box that is. Remember the study in the popular press where it was found that packaging food in a McDonald's wrapper made the food more appealing to children? Your job is to provide healthy foods that are packaged so they will actually get consumed by your picky eater. So with a great deal of fanfare, help your child select a very cool lunch box or bag to transport her food to school. Fun little containers, colorful spoons, stickers on the baggie and a note from mom can go a long way toward making your picky eater at least try to nibble on something in the lunch bag. There is nothing worse than opening the lunch bag after school and finding that the food was untouched, a common occurrence reported by many frustrated parents of children with reflux.

TIP #3: MAKE GOOD CHOICES IN THE CAFETERIA LINE

The typical school cafeteria lunch menu is full of reflux trigger foods such as greasy pizza covered in cheese and tomato sauce and fried chicken with tater tots on the side. You may need to avoid high calorie/high fat foods if your child is overweight or obese since there is some evidence that childhood obesity leads to an increase in reflux symptoms.

Most schools provide a menu in advance so you and your child can look at the options and choose foods that are tolerated. Many refluxers are such careful eaters that they wouldn't eat anything on the menu, preferring a familiar lunch from home. When my daughter Rebecca was in the middle of her picky eating phase, she would comment on the cafeteria food and mentioned that a few of the selections looked pretty appealing. I wanted her to try new foods and have the experience of buying lunch at school.

We scanned the menu and chose a day for our trial run then packed her lunch money and a light lunch as a back up. She ate a combination of the cafeteria lunch and the food from home. I know this approach is somewhat wasteful but it was important for her to have her "safe foods" if she could not tolerate the new foods. Over time, she became a regular in the cafeteria line and got to the point that she just brought water from home to substitute for the drink options that were reflux triggers for her (milk or orange juice).

TIP # 4: PUT YOUR CHILD IN CHARGE

It is likely your child will eat more of her lunch if she has packed it herself. A younger child may need to be in charge of smaller decisions. An older child may be able to select foods and prepare the entire lunch. I know a parent who keeps a lunch food chart with columns on the refrigerator. The columns represent the food groups (protein, carbs, drink, fruit and other) and acceptable choices for each category. For instance, the protein column lists: ham, chicken, protein bar, cheese, and yogurt. The drink column lists: water, sports drink or 100% fruit juice pouch. Her refluxer needs to pick an item from each column to create a well rounded lunch.

TIP #5: USE THE POWER OF PEERS TO INCREASE FOOD CHOICES

So, if you are eliminating foods that trigger reflux and foods that cause allergies and intolerances, what in the world is left? Will your carbohydrate junky live on bread, cereal and crackers forever? Definitely stock up on massive quantities of your child's preferred foods; your child may believe that only a few "safe" foods are acceptable.

Meanwhile, tap into your child's world to find ways to encourage change. Maybe your child was lucky enough to sit next to non-refluxers who eat exotic foods, like string cheese or apple slices dipped in a special sauce. Use this positive role modeling to your advantage by inviting your child to go food shopping with you and select a new food each week. I bet your child will select a food that she has seen another child eat at school. Don't worry if she selects the gummy snacks or cheese curls that are full of unknown, unhealthy ingredients. The goal is for your child to take a chance with a new food and add to her menu selections. Once she has become a bit more adventurous about new foods, you can narrow the selections to healthier foods or find a more nutritious version of the foods she has learned to eat.

Celebrate Special Occasions

Your child may find it disappointing to celebrate a holiday while on a special diet or when eating is one of the least pleasurable experiences she can imagine. But we need to press on and celebrate anyway. It is time to put on your "creativity hat" and develop a solution or a new tradition born of necessity.

To get you started, here are some approaches taken by other parents. There is no doubt you will add to the list!

For our daughter's 1st thru 4th birthdays we had a woman who makes special occasion cakes in our town make a milk/egg and soy free cake. She used egg substitute and a vanilla cake recipe from the Food Allergy Network website.

Oh, I remember the day that Emily sat in a birthday party at daycare and couldn't have a birthday cupcake because it was made with milk. She got Cheerios instead. I cried my eyes out after that, but made sure it never happened again.

We have a bakery in town that bakes dairy free cakes. So, I bought a half dozen cupcakes and kept them frozen to take in whenever the other kiddos had birthday parties so that Jenna would always have a cupcake. On her first birthday, she had the best dairy free cake. So, there are ways to get around fruit cakes and Jell-O cakes—ways to let them have a "normal" birthday cake!

Thanksgiving dinner was going just great. Rebecca ate all of the white foods-mashed potatoes, roll, and a little turkey. She would have blended in with the whole Thanksgiving scene except she couldn't leave the table without releasing one of her world-famous ten second burps!!! Then all of the comments started...

Halloween, like all holidays can be tough with reflux. My kids stray from the foods and routines that help them manage their reflux and we all have to live with the consequences. In our house, candy can be traded for money or a treat that doesn't aggravate their tummies. We save a bag of Halloween candy to decorate our Christmas gingerbread house, a family tradition.

Our daycare was wonderful when it came time for birthday parties and special occasions like Halloween and Valentine's Day. They would always include a note to all parents, reminding them that one child was "allergic to dairy and soy" and that another child was allergic to eggs. It REALLY helped out with making sure that our son got to enjoy the treats.

We are setting new traditions in our family that are not oriented around food. Instead of candy for the Christmas stockings, the children get a few small books. Instead of Easter egg hunting, we have more fun decorating the plastic eggs and hanging them on a tree.

In our house, the kids are allowed to eat as much candy as they want on Halloween night. Then it disappears so we only have one night of bellyaches.

PART 4 ▶ ADVANCED MEDICAL TOPICS

15 ▶ TESTING FOR GERD

This chapter provides you with detailed information about the tests a doctor may use to diagnose and treat Gastroesophageal Reflux Disease (GERD). It is important to understand where a test fits in the diagnosis process and why that test may or may not be indicated for your child. If your doctor has determined that a test is needed for your infant or child, it is important to read the detailed description of the test. You need to make an informed decision about giving the doctor permission to do the test and you need to prepare your little one and yourself for the test.

Upper GI Series

THE TEST

An *Upper Gastrointestinal Series* or *Upper GI* is the most common test administered to children with symptoms of reflux. The test provides a view of the digestive tract (mouth to upper intestine) to detect a structural problem such as pyloric stenosis, hiatal hernia or malrotation. An Upper GI can give a

---

> ### *Jan Says...*
>
> A mother called me in a state of confusion, right after her baby had an Upper GI Series. She reported that the radiologist said there was no evidence of reflux. How can that be? My baby clearly has all of the symptoms. I explained that the Upper GI showed that her baby didn't have a structural problem (REALLY good news) and her baby somehow managed NOT to reflux during the test. I said, "So what happened after the test was over?" She said, "Well, he vomited all over the car on the ride home." I said, "That was the reflux part."

---

rough idea if the stomach is emptying too slowly but a milk scan is a more sensitive test for this.

An Upper GI cannot diagnose reflux. Even if the child vomits during the test, it doesn't necessarily mean that the child has reflux. The child might simply have been upset and vomited. Reflux is only diagnosed based on a pattern of excessive backwashing of acid or when the backwash is causing problems.

HOW THE TEST IS DONE

An Upper GI consists of having the child drink a chalky liquid and taking an X-ray of the stomach. A normal X-ray is designed to show hard substances like bone. Soft tissues such as the stomach and intestines do not show up well on an X-ray. The chalky substance has barium in it which makes the outline of the esophagus, stomach and upper intestine easier to visualize.

WHAT YOU NEED TO KNOW:

The test will be performed on an empty stomach so you will not be able to feed your baby for several hours before the test. You may be asked to bring a bottle of her favorite formula, milk or expressed breast milk. The technicians will put barium in the bottle and ask you to feed your baby. If you are pregnant, you may need to let somebody else feed your baby and stay for the X-ray because the test involves exposure to a small amount of radiation. It might be a good idea to bring your own bottle or sippy cup to increase the chances your baby or child will drink the barium.

The barium powder tastes like chalk, but most young babies don't object much if they are hungry enough. Older children may not like the chalky feel of the barium "milk shake."

> *Just a Thought...*
>
> Being in the car seat contraption still seemed to bother him much more than it did to drink the barium and formula mixture.

Your baby may be placed on an elevated surface or wrapped on a special board or papoose to keep her from moving around too much. She might be very unhappy with this aspect of the test. The good news is parents are usually allowed to stay during the test and the test only takes a few minutes.

Wrestling your child and forcing food into her mouth may be counter-productive if she is already afraid of eating. It may actually make the situation worse if the gag reflex is stimulated and the child vomits the barium before the X-ray can be taken. The results of this struggle can be seen clearly on many X-rays - there appears to be more barium outside of the child than inside! It might be necessary to place a small tube into the child's stomach and pour the liquid through the tube.

Some parents wear a hospital gown so they are protected from vomiting during and after the test. You may want to bring a change of clothes for both of you just in case. Some children experience constipation and white, chalky stools after a test so be sure to offer extra fluids for a day or two. When the test is over, your baby can resume eating and drinking. But mostly, you will both need a good, long nap.

> ### *A GERD Mom Says...*
>
> They put a tube down his nose and throat to put the barium into his stomach. Then he was strapped to a board (while they took the X-rays) and he screamed. At least I was able to hold his hand. It broke my heart but I can assure you that two minutes after, he'd forgotten about it already. I bought him a new stuffed toy at the hospital gift shop - just to make myself feel better.

MODIFIED BARIUM SWALLOW STUDY

A swallow study is used to assess the mechanics of swallowing and evaluate a swallowing disorder, also known as dysphagia.

A swallow study is similar to an Upper GI Series. Your baby needs to drink the barium and milk mixture during the X-ray. A speech pathologist that specializes in swallowing may be in the room during the test. The swallow is recorded on video and played at slow speed to see how your baby swallows.

The test is also used for children with aspiration to see if food is entering the airway during a swallow or if the food is getting into the stomach properly but being refluxed up and getting into the lungs later.

PH Probe

THE TEST

A *pH probe* is a device that measures the acid level in the esophagus and gives an indication of reflux severity. The test also measures the frequency and duration of reflux episodes.

The probe records data and provides the doctor with detailed information about the reflux events. The data is complex and often entered into a computer scoring program to help the doctor grade the severity. For instance, if your child has one very long acid event, it may be more important than a lot of short events.

A pH probe test is considered to be an excellent test to confirm reflux; however, a few children with significant reflux have had "unremarkable" or "negative" pH probe tests on occasion.

Some doctors perform a probe while a child is on reflux medication to check the effectiveness of the treatment. Most often, the medicines are stopped a few days before the test because the goal is to see if the child has reflux without medication.

HOW THE TEST IS DONE

A thin, flexible tube is threaded up through the nose and down into the esophagus. Some pH probes have two sensors. Generally the tubing is positioned so that one probe is just above the Lower Esophageal Sphincter or LES. The other probe may be positioned in the upper esophagus or it may be positioned inside the stomach. The tube looks like aquarium tubing but as thin and flexible as al dente spaghetti with a small sensor at the end. The tubing is attached to a small box that records acid events. In general, the test takes approximately 24 hours and many hospitals require the children to stay overnight. Older children may be able to leave the hospital after the tube is inserted and go home for the duration of the test.

The probe is attached to a small box with a shoulder strap or backpack. A digital readout allows you to look at the current level of acid and get an instant reading on whether certain activities provoke reflux events. You will be asked to keep a record of food intake and activities (sitting, sleeping, and eating) throughout the test. Some parents find it overwhelming to juggle all of these duties for 24 hours.

WHAT YOU NEED TO KNOW

Your baby or child will not be allowed to eat for a few hours prior to the test. Sometimes the doctor will perform an endoscopy first and then place the pH probe while your baby is still asleep. If not, the probe will be placed while your child is awake. The placement of the tube may be the hardest part of all. While it isn't really painful to place the tube, it will be uncomfortable and scary to many children. Putting a tube in your nose just doesn't feel good. Some doctors provide a spray to numb the nose before getting started.

> ### From a GERD Mom:
>
> My toddler just had a pH probe study. The worst part was inserting the probe into his nose. I wasn't in the room but I could hear him crying from down the hall. I know he had to be held down and that sure did make him mad.

It is important for your little one to be very still for the few seconds it takes to place the probe to avoid injury. Infants and toddlers may be swaddled or placed on a special papoose to keep them from moving. A nurse may be there to keep the child still and assist the doctor with the insertion. Parents may be allowed to stay for the tube placement and can provide a soothing voice and some distraction. An X-ray is often needed to check the placement of the probe before your baby can resume eating.

Your child will also dislike the tape on his cheek to keep the tube from moving around and the irritation to his throat from the tube. She may cough and clear his throat in an attempt to adjust to the tube. In general, be prepared for a grumpy, unhappy face for the first few hours. Be sure to bring several new toys to provide a distraction.

Keeping the probe in place can be as much of a challenge as inserting it. Babies and toddlers will attempt to rub the tubing or pull it out. Mittens are routinely placed over babies' hands; most toddlers will need to wear inflatable arm splints or some other method of immobilizing the elbows so they can't reach their face. Older children may keep their hands away from the tubing if they are provided distractions such as videos and books.

A Solution:

The nurse brought mittens to put on my toddlers hands to keep her from tugging at the probe. This was clearly not enough, so we had to use arm splints that prevented her from touching her face.

Since most babies and young children are hospitalized for a pH probe, you will need to pack some essential items such as clothes, toys and food. Your baby may be able to wear regular clothes and pajamas so check with the hospital before hand so you can be prepared. It might help to bring some favorite foods and eating utensils such as bottles, sippy cups and

From a GERD Mom:

The first feeding after the insertion he vomited several times but then it did not seen to bother him too much.

familiar bibs so you can replicate diet and eating habits as much as possible. You want to have your child eat, sleep and play as normally as possible to obtain an accurate test.

At first, your baby might not want to eat because it feels strange to swallow and she might be groggy if she was sedated. A picky eater may reject everything on the hospital menu so ask the nurse for help with selecting foods. There may be a small kitchen on each floor with juice, crackers and cereal.

Jan Says...

My 5 year old was starving and eager to eat. She brightened when the tray was delivered and quickly opened the lid covering the plate. We both gasped at the same time: my world famous picky eater with severe reflux was served a southwestern omelet complete with salsa, onions and green pepper! Luckily the nurse came to our rescue and was able to get a replacement meal pretty quickly. Afterwards, I was able to laugh about it, but at the time it was not a bit funny!

◆

I found it a challenge to chase around after him in the hospital room with the pH monitor attached. The nurse told us there was a wagon we could use to take a little walk. My son was thrilled to pack up his train book and his blanket to take a "train ride." It was a relief to keep him busy and distracted, even for a few minutes.

You and your child should be able to visit the playroom and perhaps even go to other parts of the hospital such as the gift shop or cafeteria. While you probably don't want to encourage gymnastics, you should certainly be as active as possible.

Upper Endoscopy

THE TEST

An endoscope is a flexible tube attached to a small camera that allows a doctor to see into the body. It allows the doctor to view the walls of the esophagus, stomach and the upper part of the intestine.

HOW THE TEST IS DONE

An *endoscopy* is usually done in a procedure room with IV sedation. Some children with respiratory issues may require general anesthesia. During the test, the end of the scope is carefully pushed into the mouth and down the esophagus. The doctor will advance the scope slowly and watch on a video monitor. When an area of concern is viewed, a camera or a video tape can be used to record the image. An endoscope lets the gastroenterologist observe visible damage to the esophagus such as swelling, scaring or ulcerations. The scope can also be used to view problems in the stomach such as ulcers or gastritis.

WHAT YOU NEED TO KNOW

The hardest part of an endoscopy for your child is the test preparation and sedation. There may be some discomfort from inserting an IV for fluids and medicine as well as anxiety about the test.

Procedures for preparing a child for sedation vary from hospital to hospital. A child may receive medication to relax her and make her drowsy. The doctor may use a mask to provide a small amount of medication to make the child fall asleep for a few minutes. To make it more appealing to a child, the masks often smell like fruit or bubble gum. Some doctors wait until the child is asleep to start an IV while others insert an IV when the child is awake.

After the test it will be necessary for your child to stay for a period of observation. Your child will be offered a drink and you will probably go home with instructions to resume eating and activity as tolerated.

BIOPSY

Some types of damage may not be visible to the naked eye so biopsies (small samples of tissue) will be taken during the endoscopy to check for microscopic damage, signs of allergies and the bacteria that cause ulcers.

One common change is the presence of while blood cells called *eosinophils*. These cells belong in the blood stream, not in the digestive system. The significance of eosinophils in the digestive system is not entirely clear. Eosinophils in the esophagus are believed by some doctors to indicate that acid exposure has occurred and the eosinophils are present as a part of the healing process. However, dramatically elevated eosinophils may trigger a diagnosis of Eosinophilic Esophagitis, a condition that is related to food allergies and appears to be increasing dramatically in children.

Biopsies are one way of testing for the presence of helicobacter pylori, the bacteria implicated in ulcers. The significance of an h.Pylori test is the subject of much debate.

Biopsies are also used to check for cellular changes that can occur as a result of chronic damage.

Food Allergy Testing

Our understanding of allergies and food intolerances has changed dramatically in the past few years as researchers learn more about how and why food reactions occur.

It is important to find an allergist who likes to work with food mediated allergies and who has experience working with infants and young children. There are societies of allergists and several patient support groups that may be able to help you learn more about current allergy theories.

TESTING METHODS

Skin tests are the most common test for food allergies. A drop of food is applied to the child's back and then scratched lightly into the skin. After a period of time, the skin is checked for redness or hives (raised itchy spots).

A GERD Mom Says...

My son's reflux is absolutely allergy driven. When I was nursing, I eliminated milk, eggs, soy, nuts, chocolate, beef and several other foods. It was a huge amount of work and the pediatrician didn't think it was worth it. As far as we are concerned, it is worth the expense and work.

Patch tests are a type of skin testing that may demonstrate "slow" allergies. It involves saturating a small band aid with a food and sticking it on the patient for several days.

RAST and ELISA are special blood tests and may be an option to test for food allergies. Some patients prefer a single blood test over a skin test involving multiple pricks/scratches. They may not be as accurate for every type of allergy.

Elimination diet is another strategy to "test" for food allergies. Under the supervision of a doctor, a strict diet is adhered to for a short time (7-14 day). After a week or more, one food or food group is added back to the diet. The theory is if the symptoms go away when a food or food group is taken out of the diet, the food was the cause of the symptoms. Likewise, if you add the food back to the diet after the trial and symptoms return, it confirms the role of the food in causing symptoms. An elimination diet requires a great deal of work and vigilance to implement, but can be well worth the effort.

Scintigraphy, Scintiscan, Milk Scan or Gastric Emptying Test

THE TEST

Scintigraphy or a *scintiscan* is often referred to as a milk scan or delayed emptying test. The test can detect reflux but it is more often used to track the progress of food as it moves out of the stomach (gastric emptying) and through the digestive system. A doctor may also use scintigraphy to detect aspiration of food into the lungs.

WHAT YOU NEED TO KNOW

The test is performed in the nuclear medicine department or radiology department. The radiologist will place a small amount of radioactive material in a drink you provide (milk, formula or breast milk). Your child needs to drink at least 2-4 ounces for the test to be reliable. Older children may be given food instead of a liquid.

Some parents are concerned about the idea of their baby or child ingesting the radioactive material for the test. You need to know that the material is excreted when the child has a bowel movement and does not stay in the body permanently.

214

To conduct the test, it is necessary for the child to lie still for about an hour while a series of images are taken. An infant or toddler may need to be swaddled or strapped onto a papoose board to keep them from moving. A blanket or pacifier may be helpful for an infant. An older child may be able to cooperate and lie still on the table for the duration of the test when provided ear phones for music or other distraction. Some testing facilities have TV's and videos for the children to watch. It is always a good idea to bring your own bag of tricks—a book, earphones or music.

After the first hour of testing, your child can get up for a break and move about. Unfortunately, the test has two parts so she will need to go back on the table again. Luckily the second half of the test is a lot shorter.

It is likely your baby or toddler will think this test is a very bad idea and may cry and carry on. You can ask for medication to help her relax. If you are lucky, your little one will fall into an exhausted sleep at some point.

Less Common Tests

DUAL CHANNEL PH PROBE

Many hospitals are purchasing probes with two sensors. A *Dual Channel pH Probe* can be particularly useful if the child has confusing symptoms. One probe can be placed in the lower esophagus and one in the stomach if   reflux is suspected. Sometimes the two probes are positioned so one is in the lower esophagus and one is in the upper esophagus. This helps to detect whether the acid is getting all the way up into the mouth or airway.

MULTI-CHANNEL INTRALUMINAL IMPEDANCE

The Multi Channel Intraluminal Impedance Test (MMI) is a newer, more sophisticated version of a pH probe which can sense acid and nonacid events. Unfortunately, it is not widely available at this time.

While a traditional pH probe may have two sensors, the MMI has sensors along the length of the tubing. These special sensors can detect the difference between food that is being swallowed (going down) and food that is being refluxed (going up). It is also possible to detect liquid in the esophagus and episodes of reflux that are not acidic. It is believed that non-acid reflux can still cause problems such as pain and choking for some children.

PHARYNGEAL AIRWAY pH MONITOR

A new device is available that monitors acid vapors at the back of the mouth near the airway.

ESOPHAGEAL MANOMETRY

Manometry is a test to diagnose children with complications including swallowing disorders or an overly tight Lower Esophageal Sphincter (achalasia). A small flexible tube is placed in the esophagus and measures the strength of the muscle contractions that move food through the digestive system. The child may be asked to drink or swallow during the test.

LACTOSE AND OTHER SUGAR INTOLERANCE TESTS

Lactose intolerance is a condition characterized by gas, bloating and diarrhea. It is caused by the inability to digest lactose, a digestive sugar that naturally occurs in milk. An inability to digest sugars such as lactose, fructose, mannitol, and sorbitol may cause digestive discomfort that may be confused with reflux symptoms. Lactose intolerance is rather uncommon in infants and toddlers. Older children may be tested using an elimination diet or a breath hydrogen test. There are many lactose free foods and formulas as well as over-the-counter medications which help break down lactose.

GLUTEN INTOLERANCE TEST

An inability to digest gluten found in wheat, barley, rye and oats may indicate Celiac Disease. However, the symptoms of Celiac Disease may look like reflux in the early stages. If a child is intolerant of gluten, further testing may be warranted including blood tests or a biopsy.

SWEAT TEST

A Sweat Test determines if an infant or child has Cystic Fibrosis (CF). Cystic Fibrosis is a rare condition characterized by severe breathing and digestive problems causing poor weight gain. Since some children with GERD also have

> ### *Jan says:*
>
> When the pulmonologist said she needed a test for Cystic Fibrosis I was shocked. The doctor saw the panicked look on my face and quickly added that it was highly unlikely she had CF. The doctor explained that CF is extremely rare but early detection is very important. Of course the test came out negative. I think they call it a "sweat test" because it makes the parents so worried that they start to perspire!

respiratory problems and asthma, a sweat test may be performed as a precaution to rule out CF. During a sweat test, a child's perspiration is collected on absorbent pads and then tested for certain types of salt.

16 ▶ COMMONLY USED GERD MEDICATIONS

It may be alarming to read the list of potential side effects of the medications in this chapter. Keep in mind that most babies and children tolerate medication; side effects are mild and often go away after the body has adjusted to the medication. A list of side effects is provided so you will be aware of common and uncommon responses to medication.

If you look on the label of any medication, you will see a long list of documented side effects. When a drug is being tested, any illness or symptom that occurs during the study is noted. If a child happens to have an ear infection while she is in a study for a new reflux medication, ear infections could come up as a "side effect" of taking the medication. If you observe new symptoms or possible side effects from a medication, it is always best to consult with your doctor right away.

Over the past few decades, there have been many changes in the way children with reflux are medicated. In the late 1980s, the medicines that were in common use were antacids and H2 blockers. These gave way to motility medications which held great promise because they seemed to address the underlying cause of reflux in children, spontaneous Lower Esophageal Sphincter (LES) relaxation. Unfortunately, dangerous side effects were discovered with the most common motility medication and this whole class of medications is no longer in wide use. Soon a new class of medications, the *Proton Pump Inhibitor* or *PPIs* came into use, first for adults, and later for children. They address the problem from a different angle – they suppress acid rather than improving the muscle tone. In the next decade or so, the trend will probably change again as newer medications come on the market.

H2 Blockers

Acid suppressors reduce reflux symptoms by reducing stomach acid production. *H2 blockers* interfere with the effect of one type of histamine and may offer a small amount of additional protection for those with food allergies.

Brand Names (USA)	Generic Name
Axid	Nizatidine
Pepcid, Mylanta AR	Famotidine
Tagamet plus generics	Cimetidine
Zantac plus generics	Ranitidine

WHAT YOU NEED TO KNOW

Acid suppressors can be given "as needed" or daily for long-term relief of symptoms. Acid suppressors are generally given several times per day. They can be taken with food but are more effective when taken on an empty stomach.

H2 blockers may interact with PPIs so they should be given at separate times of day. H2 blockers may also affect the absorption of other medicines, particularly those that need acid to be metabolized properly. Check with your pharmacist. The doctor may increase the dose of H2 blockers as the child grows.

Some patients develop a tolerance to these medicines and they stop working. Switching brands may help. Some patients report rebound acid when these medicines are stopped abruptly. It may be better to wean off them.

SIDE EFFECTS

Keep in mind that most babies and children tolerate medication; side effects are mild and often go away after the body has adjusted to the medication. A list of side effects is provided so you will be aware of common and uncommon responses to medication.

H2 blockers can cause headaches, dizziness, nausea, constipation, diarrhea or stomach pain. Agitation and confusion have been reported as well as nightmares and night terrors. Rare side effects include the possibility of a higher incidence of pneumonia and gastrointestinal infections.

Use of H2 blockers could theoretically reduce absorption of iron and vitamin B 12 causing anemia or pernicious anemia.

Proton Pump Inhibitors

A *Proton Pump Inhibitor (PPI)* is a medication that inhibits acid production in the stomach. Most proton pump inhibitors are time released meaning the medication is slowly released into the body, offering long term relief of symptoms.

Brand Names (USA)	Generic Name
AcipHex	Rabeprazole
Nexium	Esomeprazole
Prevacid	Lansoprozole
Prilosec	Omeprazole
Protonix	Pantoprazole
Zegerid	Omeprazole
Many non-prescription brands	Omeprazole

WHAT YOU NEED TO KNOW:

A PPI should be given approximately 30 minutes before a meal on an empty stomach for maximum effectiveness.

New research shows that some children metabolize the medication very rapidly and may need several small doses rather than one large dose. Children age 1-10 often need doses that are larger for their weight than an adult would need.

Studies show that discontinuing PPIs abruptly may cause the stomach to make higher amounts of acid. This rebound effect may be avoided by tapering doses rather than stopping suddenly.

Different brands come in different formulations: tablet, capsule, time release capsule, melt on the tongue tablet, powder and liquid. This variety should help you and your doctor find a formulation that is tolerated by your child. It is important to use each formulation the way the doctor and the pharmacist tell you to ensure that the medicine is absorbed effectively. The manufacturers have hotlines to answer questions about how to administer their medicines correctly. Flavoring and compounding must also be done carefully according to strict recipes.

SIDE EFFECTS

Keep in mind that most babies and children tolerate medication; side effects are mild and often go away after the body has adjusted to the medication. A list of side effects is provided so you will be aware of common and uncommon responses to medication.

PPIs can cause headaches, diarrhea, nausea and constipation. There may be a higher incidence of pneumonia and gastrointestinal infections in patients on PPIs.

Use of PPIs could theoretically reduce absorption of iron and vitamin B 12 causing anemia or pernicious anemia.

Long term use of PPIs could theoretically unbalance the beneficial bacteria in the digestive system.

Some parents report that PPI medication may cause spit up to have a purple color.

CAUTION

PPIs may affect the absorption of other medicines, particularly those that need acid to be metabolized properly.

These are strong medications and should be used cautiously and only when necessary. There is some evidence that suggests newborns and young babies may not have the digestive enzymes to break down this type of medication. However, most data shows that infants and young children metabolize these medications more rapidly than adults.

Antacids

Antacids are often used by adults to treat mild reflux and quickly neutralize acid that is already present in the stomach. Antacids work very quickly and come in many flavors and forms – look for tiny pills that can be swallowed or chewed and even sprinkles/powders. Antacids are inexpensive and don't require a prescription but they are hard on the kidneys. The North American Society for Pediatric Gastroenterology, Hepatology and Nutrition does not recommend the use of antacids for long term treatment of reflux in children. A doctor may suggest a short trial of antacids to see if reflux symptoms resolve and confirm a suspected diagnosis of reflux.

Brand Names (USA)	Main Ingredient
Tums	Calcium
Maalox	Aluminum and magnesium
Children's Mylanta	Calcium
Rolaids	Calcium and magnesium
Milk of Magnesia	Magnesium
Prelief	Calcium
Gaviscon	Aluminum and a foaming barrier agent
Children's Pepto Bismol	Calcium. Adult versions contain Bismuth subsalicylate, a chemical similar to aspirin and should not be used for children.
Alka Seltzer	Contains aspirin and should not be used for children.

WHAT YOU NEED TO KNOW

Antacids are typically used for children with occasional bouts of reflux or used on days when a prescription medicine isn't enough.

SIDE EFFECTS

A list of common and uncommon possible side effects is provided. Keep in mind that most infants and children tolerate antacids when used as directed by their physician.

Antacids with magnesium tend to cause diarrhea. Antacids with aluminum tend to be constipating. None are safe to use at high doses for prolonged periods of time. Always consult your physician before administering an over-the-counter medication to your child. Even antacids can be dangerous to give without medical supervision. There is some concern that antacids containing aluminum may inhibit calcium and zinc absorption.

Antacids may contain artificial sweeteners that are not tolerated or sugar that can cause cavities.

Physical Barriers

Physical barriers may protect the esophagus and stomach from damage by providing *a coating or barrier from acid exposure.* The medication also floats on top of stomach contents and may provide a physical barrier to keep acid from backwashing into the esophagus.

This type of medication may be used to promote healing of the esophagus as well as to treat ulcers. A physical barrier can provide immediate relief from symptoms and very little is absorbed into the body.

There is little or no evidence that these medications reduce reflux symptoms or protect the esophagus from damage but many patients report symptom relief. Brand names are *Carafate (sucralfate)* and *Gaviscon (Alginic Acid Slurry).*

WHAT YOU NEED TO KNOW

Usually, this medication is given prior to a meal. The tablets can be easily dissolved in water.

SIDE EFFECTS

A list of common and uncommon possible side effects is provided. Keep in mind that most infants and children tolerate physical barriers when used as directed.

Constipation is the only common side effect. *Sulcrafate* has properties similar to glue and rare reports exist of food balls (bezoars) which are somewhat similar to hair balls.

CAUTION

Typically a physical barrier should not be administered at the same time as other medications that rely upon absorption because they will probably bind to these medications.

Motility Medications

Motility medications or *Prokinetics* move food through the digestive tract more effectively and a bit faster by enhancing stomach emptying speeds. This type of medication will improve esophageal clearance of reflux events and tighten the Lower Esophageal Sphincter. Motility drugs may be used for delayed emptying of the stomach and aspiration from reflux.

Brand Names	Generic Name
Propulsid	Cisapride
Bethanacol	Urecholine
Reglan	Metoclopramide
Motilium	Domperidone (not available in USA)
Many	Erythromycin
Milk of Magnesia	Magnesium
Baclofen	Lioresal

WHAT YOU NEED TO KNOW

All motility medications have a history of side effects and there is little research to support their usefulness in treatment. Doctors are using them with a great deal of caution and looking forward to the newer motility medications that are currently being developed by several manufacturers.

Metaclopramide (Reglan) is in a class of medications called *neuroleptics* which are used for control of vomiting as well as delayed gastric emptying. Metaclopramide has fallen out of favor due to the side effects and the mixed evidence about its effectiveness.

Bethanechol (Urecholine) is a medicine to help the bladder empty. Because it works to constrict muscles in the digestive system, it can be used to improve motility. Bethanechol must be compounded for use with children. The compound has a short shelf life making it difficult to use.

SIDE EFFECTS

Motility medications have been associated with mild to severe side effects. When used with proper care and monitoring infants and children may tolerate motility medications and benefit from reduced symptoms. Motility medications have been known to cause abdominal cramps and diarrhea so the dose is often started low and increased slowly. A complete list of common and uncommon side effects is provided.

Side effects of *Metoclopramide* include: restlessness, fatigue, agitation, insomnia, headache, confusion and dizziness. Metoclopramide can cause serious neurological side effects, particularly in children. Parents need to discuss the side effects of this medication with the physician and pharmacist and weigh the benefit of using the medication vs. the potential for side effects. If your child is on this medication, ask for a list of the side effects so you can help watch for emerging problems.

Bethanechol can cause bronchial constrictions and asthma attacks, a rapid heart rate, low blood pressure, whole body discomfort like the flu, abdominal cramps, nausea, belching, a sensation of overheating, constriction of the pupils and watery eyes.

Cisapride (Propulsid) was used widely in the United States in the past. It appears to be an effective motility medication but it caused abnormal heart arrhythmias in some patients. After several deaths were reported, the Food and Drug Administration removed Cisapride from the market in the United States. It is still available for some patients under strict guidelines including EKG monitoring.

The current formulation of *Lioresal* is sedating and may be habit forming, however, it is being reformulated. Lioresal is actually an anti-spasmodic that can be beneficial in reducing the number of inappropriate relaxations of the Lower

Esophageal Sphincter. At present, this medication is most often used to treat children with muscle spasticity in addition to reflux.

Medications for Related Symptoms
ANTI GAS MEDICATIONS

Anti gas medications reduce digestive gas production and disperse gas bubbles. While this class of medications is not truly a treatment for reflux, many babies experience painful burping and gas during and after a meal. While there is little evidence that these medications work, some parents report that these medications relieve symptoms with no known side effects. The generic name of this medication is *Simethicone* with several brand names including: Gas-X, Mylanta Gas, Mylicon Drops and Phazyme.

MEDICATION TO INCREASE APPETITE

A medication to make your baby feel hungry or increase appetite is referred to as an appetite stimulant. *Periactin (Cyproheptadine)* is an appetite stimulant that is sometimes used as a short term treatment to boost oral intake. Side effects may include: dizziness, sleepiness, agitation and irritability.

17 ▶WHEN SURGERY IS NECESSARY

Medical treatment successfully controls the symptoms and complications of GERD in the vast majority of infants and children. Infants and children faced with multiple treatments, lifelong medication therapy or who fail to get adequate symptom relief from medical treatment and medications may be a candidate for surgery. It is important to remember that surgery is an uncommon treatment for GERD and is used only for a small number of cases. It is estimated that several million children in the United States have GERD but only a few thousand surgical procedures for GERD are performed each year. Many parents worry needlessly about the surgery even when it is not indicated.

When Surgery Is the Best Option

There are several surgical options but the *Nissen Fundoplication* is the most common surgical procedure for the treatment of Gastroesophageal Reflux Disease in all age groups. Most surgeons perform the surgery using a less evasive laparoscopic method. During laparoscopic surgery, several small incisions are made into the abdomen (stomach) and small instruments are used to perform the surgery. A very small baby may need to have one large incision called an *Open Nissen Fundoplication*. In either case, the top of the stomach is wrapped around the base of the esophagus and stitched into place. Some surgeons have been trained in the *Thal Fundoplication* or the *Toupet Fundoplication* (partial wrap). The *Toupet* has a reduced rate of complications from gas bloat and swallowing issues but may not be as effective for severe reflux.

Parents are often discouraged to find that the newer, non surgical (less evasive) procedures for treating GERD are not available for infants and children. As of this writing, the other non surgical methods are still being refined for adult use so parents should not delay surgery in hopes of finding an alternative treatment in the near future.

INDICATIONS FOR SURGERY

An evaluation by a pediatric gastroenterologist is essential in determining the extent of the reflux and exploring all medical treatments before referring a child for surgery. A pediatric gastroenterologist may perform tests that provide vital information to the surgeon who must make the ultimate decision on whether a child is a good candidate for surgery.

Surgery may be indicated if your child has one or more of the following complications from reflux and treatment failed to control her symptoms.

Esophagitis, **a significant irritation and scarring from acid exposure.**
Apnea
Failure to thrive
Pneumonia **from aspiration of food/stomach contents into the lungs**
Asthma **from irritation to the lungs from reflux episodes**
Airway damage
Strictures **– narrowing of the esophagus**
Barrett's Esophagus
*ALTE's***—Apparent Life Threatening Events**
Medical treatment failure
Significant quality of life issues
Significant oral motor disorders

FINDING A SURGEON

It is important to find a pediatric surgeon having a great deal of experience with GERD surgery. A surgeon who is familiar with the procedure and performs the procedure on a regular basis will have the skill and practice to perfect the technique. Further, a surgeon who is familiar with pediatric gastroesophageal reflux disease will know the importance of scheduling tests before the surgery to assess the severity of the reflux and the seriousness of the complication that warrant surgery. In my experience, it is a myth that surgeons want to perform a *Nissen Fundoplication* on every baby or child referred for surgery. In fact, surgeons are quite careful about determining that the surgery will benefit the child before making a recommendation.

Parents often want to know where the best surgeon is so they can fly across the country or the world. The reality is, the Nissen Fundoplication surgery is a common pediatric surgery procedure in the United States so it is unnecessary to travel very far to find a surgeon who can perform the procedure. It makes sense to consult the pediatric gastroenterologist and the pediatrician first since they are familiar with local surgeons and hospitals with pediatric care units. In addition, some parents prefer to travel to a large city to obtain care at a large regional children's hospital. It is important to find a surgeon who you feel comfortable with. Some parents look for a surgeon with a good reputation while others need a doctor who will answer the questions on the two page list you brought to the appointment and follow up by phone as needed.

QUESTIONS TO ASK THE GASTROENTEROLOGIST AND SURGEON:

Parents will have many questions about the indicators for surgery as well as about the procedure.

You may want to ask the doctor:

Is the reflux causing damage that is not reversible?
Is the reflux causing life threatening symptoms?
Is there an immediate need for surgery or is there time to explore options?
Have all mediations and combinations been thoroughly explored?
What is known at the present time about the long term affects of the medications?
Is my child young enough that the reflux can still be expected to resolve?

Has testing shown reflux or the symptoms of reflux?
Have there been contradictory test results?
Have any tests been suggestive of another medical problem?
**Have other conditions that cause reflux symptoms been fully
  ruled out?**

Sometimes, the doctors and specialists don't agree on the need for surgery. This can be very confusing to a parent. Don't be discouraged by the mixed messages. Doctors base their decisions on their training and experience and often there are many equally good ways to treat the same problem. As a parent, you will need to sort through all of the data and recommendations to decide on a treatment plan. It may help to get a second opinion from another specialist or surgeon before proceeding.

Doctors and parents will weigh the impact of the medical condition with the impact on quality of life. Regardless of the severity of the symptoms and health issues, the medical team and the family will exhaust every treatment option before considering a surgical procedure for GERD. The doctor and surgeon will want to rule out other conditions that may impact the success of the surgery such as delayed gastric emptying and food allergies.

You and your child may tolerate significant lifestyle modifications with all the extra steps involved to avoid surgery. Others find that chronic pain and illnesses coupled with extra caretaking (night waking, special food preparation, etc) and long term medication dependency (with unknown consequences) makes surgery look like an option worth considering.

Ultimately, you will need to decide if surgery is the best option for your child after hearing the recommendations of the specialists and the surgeon. It may be helpful to use family, friends or a patient support network to share ideas and worries about the procedure. They know you and your child well and can help you sort out your questions and concerns about the surgery. In addition, it may be important to have a follow up meeting or phone call with the surgeon to clear up any questions or concerns.

SCARY SURGERY STORIES ON THE INTERNET

Reflux surgery is fairly common and has a good track record for success. However, there are many strongly worded messages floating around the Web about *Nissen Fundoplication* and other procedures to treat reflux.

You may have heard or read: "The surgery made my child worse"; or perhaps, "The surgery caused new problems"; or "My child still needs reflux medication and still refluxes every day."

Focusing on all the worst case scenarios may lead you to believe that the surgery doesn't really have a good success rate and isn't worth the risk.

It is important to remember that all surgical procedures carry some risk ranging from mild, temporary symptoms to a worsening of the medical condition. For some children, reflux surgery can be a life saving procedure. For others, it can be a cure, allowing a child to grow and develop without long term consequences. The parents who report post-surgical complications represent the minority of possible outcomes. The problems are real and surgery can cause new serious health issues. However, one must consider what the outcome would be if the child didn't have surgery. It is likely that there would be serious implications for not doing surgery as well.

The reality is, most children benefit from the surgery and have a good outcome. The parents of the kids who had a successful surgery are unlikely to be the parents staying up late to relay their story on an internet discussion board. In all likelihood, these parents are sleeping all night, enjoying the web to register their now healthy kids for the soccer team rather than describing in great detail how successful the surgery was. We will never hear their full story. They are too busy chasing their healthy kids around and recovering from a difficult season of parenthood. Occasionally, they will admire the surgical scars as a distant reminder of their former lives, now faded and faint.

Parents who want to research the medical literature for information about the surgery and the success rate are faced with hundreds of studies and many, many different criteria for "success." One study may look at quality of life as criteria for success while others will look at need for medication, return of symptoms, decrease in cough and asthma, pH levels pre and post surgery and endoscopy findings. Be sure to ask the surgeon for information on outcomes and risks.

After the Surgery

In the hospital, your child will be given strong pain relief and an IV for nourishment. There may be some tubes and drains as well. As she feels better, pain medication will be decreased and food intake will begin. First, clear liquids and soft food are introduced since the esophagus will be swollen and choking may occur.

Be sure to stay in the hospital until you feel confident in home care and your child is able to eat and drink enough to stay hydrated. Most children need to restrict their activities for a few weeks and slowly increase their diet to more solid foods.

TUBE FEEDING

Your child may have a gastrostomy tube placed during the surgery for releasing (called venting) air in the stomach or if there is a history of aspiration, feeding aversion or nutrition issues. A small incision is made into the wall of the stomach and a thin, flexible gastrostomy tube is inserted. The incision heals quickly and a small one-way valve called a button is placed in the opening. A button is very small and not as bulky as having a tube hanging under the clothing at all times. With a button, a removable tube can be attached and used as needed. Liquid nutrition and medications can be poured down a large syringe (called a bolus feeding) or a feeding pump can be attached to the tubing so that formula can be dripped into the stomach at a predetermined rate and speed. When the tube is no longer needed for venting or nutrition, it can be taken out and the small hole will usually close on it's own in a few days to a few weeks.

COMMON POST-SURGERY ISSUES

Before you leave the hospital, the surgeon will give you instructions on home care and signs of complications. Fever, pain and discharge from the incision are common warning signs that need to be reported to the doctor right away. Your doctor will tell you how to contact the surgery staff if needed.

The most common post surgery problems are swallowing issues, retching and gas bloat or the build up of air in the stomach. Most of these problems resolve over time with careful home care including: eating a liquid or soft diet, chopping food, eating slowly, eating small, frequent meals and chewing well.

Rare complications of surgery include dumping syndrome, the rapid release of stomach contents into the intestines. This produces strong nausea often accompanied by sweating, weakness and diarrhea.

Adhesions are bands of scar tissue that cause the walls of the stomach to stick to other nearby organs. This is a rare complication of any abdominal surgery that becomes more common with multiple surgeries. Symptoms include failure to pass a stool, extreme cramping, pain, bloating and dehydration.

►RESOURCES

Books

Allergy Cooking with Ease **(2001)**
Nicolette Dumke
Starburst Publishing

Digestive Wellness **(1999)**
Elizabeth Lipski, MS, CCN.
Keats Publishing

The Attachment Parenting Book **(2001)**
Bill and Martha Sears
Little Brown and Company

The Family Nutrition Book **(2005)**
Bill and Martha Sears
Little Brown and Company

The Baby Book **(1993)**
Bill and Martha Sears
Little Brown & Company

The Fussy Baby Book **(1996)**
Bill and Martha Sears
Little Brown and Company

Colic Solved **(2007)**
Bryan Vartabedian, MD
Ballantine Books

Coping with Chronic Heartburn *(2001)*
Elaine Fantle Shimberg
St. Martin's Griffin

The Happiest Baby on the Block *(2002)*
Harvey Karp, MD
Bantam Books

How to Get Your Baby to Sleep *(2002)*
Bill and Martha Sears
Little Brown and Company

Just Take a Bite *(2005)*
Lori Ernsperger and Tania Stegen-Hanson
Future Horizons

Life on the Reflux Rollercoaster *(2001)*
Roni MacLean and Jean McNeil
Publish America

Making Life Better for a Child with Acid Reflux *(2006)*
Mike and Tracy Davenport
Sportwork, Inc.

Milk Soy Protein Intolerance Guidebook/Cookbook *(2001)*
Tamara Field

Nighttime Parenting: How to get Your Baby and Child to Sleep *(1999)*
Bill and Martha Sears.
Le Leche League International Book

Poor Eaters - Helping Children who Refuse to Eat *(1990)*
Joel Macht, PhD.
Perseus Publishing

Secrets of the Baby Whisperer: How to Calm, Connect, and Communicate with Your Baby *(2005)*
Tracy Hoggs
Atria Books

Products
FEEDING

Adiri
110 Vista Centre Drive
Forest, Virginia 24551
888-768-4459
www.adiri.com

Dr. Brown's Natural Flow Bottle
Handi-Craft Company
4433 Fyler Avenue
St. Louis, Missouri 63116
1-800-778-9001
info@handi-craft.com

New Visions
Mealtimes Catalog
1124 Roberts Mountain Road
Faber, Virginia 22938
800-606-7112
www.new-vis.com

Thick-It
Precision Foods
St Louis, Missouri
1-800-431-1119 or 1-877-751-5095
www.thickitretail.com

Positioning

Amby Baby Motion Bed (Amby Baby USA)
10285 Yellow Circle Dr.
Minneapolis, MN 55343
952-974-5100 or 1-866-516-baby
www.ambybaby.com

AR Pillow, Inc
80 Bar Beach Road
Port Washington, New York 11050
917-699-0608
www.arpillow.com

Comfort Lift Bed
Comfort Lift Pillow Company, Inc
3691 Inca Street
Robstown, Texas 78380
361-767-1888
refluxpillow@yahoo.com

Medslant
800-346-1850
www.medslant.com

Pollywog Nursing Positioner
Pollywog Baby, Inc.
5710 NE 56th St
Seattle, WA 98105
1-866-332-0958
www.pollywogbaby.com

Tucker Sling
Tucker Designs, Inc
P.O. Box 641117
Kenner, Louisiana 70064
888-236-9275
www.tuckerdesigns.com

Patient Information

Carolina Pediatric Dysphagia
1110 Navaho Drive
Raleigh, NC 27609
www.feeding.com

Children's Digestive Health and Nutrition Foundation (CDHNF)
P.O. Box 6
Flourtown, Pennsylvania 19031
215-233-0808
www.cdhnf.org

Pediatric Encouragement Feeding Program
Kluge Children's Rehabilitation Program
2270 Ivy Road
Charlottesville, VA 22903
www.healthsystem.virginia.edu

National Digestive Diseases Information Clearinghouse
2 Information Way
Bethesda, MD, 20892-3570
800-891-5389
www.digestive.niddk.nih.gov

National Institute of Diabetes and Digestive and Kidney Diseases (NIDDK)
31 Center Drive
Bethesda, MD, 20892-2560
301-496-3583
www.niddk.nih.gov

Parent Support

Allergy and Asthma Network/Mothers of Asthmatics
2751 Prosperity Avenue, Suite 150
Fairfax, Virginia 22031
800-878-4403
www.aanma.org

American Partnership for Eosinophilic Disorders
(APFED)
3419 Whispering Way Drive
Richmond, Texas 77469
713-498-8216
www.apfed.org

The HealthCentral Network
1655 North Fort Myers Drive
Arlington, Virginia 22209
www.healthcentral.com/acid-reflux

EA/TEF Child and Family Support Connection, Inc.
(Esophageal Atresia, Tracheo-Esophageal Fistula)
111 West Jackson Boulevard
Suite 1145
Chicago, IL 60604-3502
(312)987-9085
www.eatef.org

Food Allergy and Anaphylaxis Network
11781 Lee Jackson Hwy., Suite 160
Fairfax, VA 22033-3309
800-929-4040
www.foodallergy.org

La Leche League International
1400 N. Meacham Road
Schaumburg, IL, 60173
847- 519-7730
www.lalecheleague.org

Kids with Food Allergies
73 Old Dublin Pike, Suite 10-163
Doylestown, PA 18901
215-230-5394
www.kidswithfoodallergies.org

National Organization for Rare Disorders
55 Kenosia Avenue
PO Box 1968
Danbury, CT 06813-1968
203- 744-0100
800-999-6673 (voicemail only)
orphan@rarediseases.org

Pediatric Adolescent Gastroesophageal Reflux Association
P.O. Box 486
Buckeystown, Maryland 21717
301-601-9541
www.reflux.org

Oley Foundation (Tube Feeding Support)
Albany Medical Center, 214 Hun Memorial, A-28
Albany, NY 12208-3478
1-800-776-OLEY
1-518-262-5079 (Outside USA)
www.oley.org

Professional Organizations

American Academy of Allergy, Asthma & Immunology
555 East Wells Street, Suite 1100
Milwaukee, WI 53202-3823
Phone: 414-272-6071
Patient Information and Physician Referral Line: 800-822-2762
www.aaaai.org

American Academy of Pediatrics
141 Northwest Point Boulevard
P.O. Box 927
Elk Grove Village, IL 60009-0927
847-228-5005
www.aap.org

American College of Allergy, Asthma & Immunology
85 West Algonquin Road, Suite 550
Arlington Heights, IL 60005
www.acaai.org

American College of Gastroenterology
P.O. Box 3099
Alexandria, VA 22302
703-820-7400
www.acg.org

North American Society for Pediatric Gastroenterology, Hepatology, and Nutrition (NASPGHAN)
PO Box 6
Flourtown, PA 19031
215-233-0808
www.naspghan.org

Travel Assistance for Medical Care

Angel Flight
3161 Donald Douglas Loop South
Santa Monica, CA 90405
888-4-AN-ANGEL
info@angelflight.org

National Association of Hospital Hospitality Houses, Inc. (NAHHH).
P.O. Box 18087
Asheville, NC 28814-0087
1-800-542-9730
www.nahhh.org

PatientTravel.org
% Mercy Medical Airlift
4620 Haygood Road, Ste. 1
Virginia Beach, VA 23455
Phone: 757-318-9174; Patient HELPLINE: 1-800-296-1217
www.mercymedical.org

Family/Care Giver Support

Starbright Foundation
1850 Sawtelle Blvd, Suite 450
Los Angeles, CA 90025
310-479-1212
800-315-2580
www.starbright.org

► MEET THE AUTHOR

Jan Gambino, M.Ed.

Jan Gambino graduated from Boston University with a B.S. degree in Special Education and Elementary Education. She completed her Masters degree in Early Childhood/Special Education at the University of North Carolina at Chapel Hill. She has over 15 years experience working with medically fragile, developmentally delayed infants and preschoolers.

Jan received intense, on the job training in parenting a child with reflux followed the birth of her youngest daughter, diagnosed with severe GERD and asthma. This led to her involvement in the Pediatric Adolescent Gastroesophageal Reflux Association (PAGER Association), where she served as Associate Director for 6 years. Throughout her sojourn as associate director and now as writer of a weekly blog on all aspects of parenting a child with reflux for *The HealthCentral Network*, Jan has offered information and guidance to hundreds of parents worldwide who have contacted her.

Jan has also written numerous brochures and booklets about parenting a child with Gastroesophageal Reflux Disease for the PAGER Association including: *Going to School with Acid Reflux*, *GERD 101*, *Feeding Your Child with Reflux*, *Dental Care for the Child with Acid Reflux*, *Teen Symptoms* and *Teen 411*. She has published articles on pediatric reflux in *Asthma and Allergy Today* and *Exceptional Parent* magazine.

Jan lives in Maryland with her three daughters and two cats. She spends most of her time "spewing" helpful and graphic information about gastroesophageal reflux to friends and strangers. Watch for her van with the vanity plates GERDMOM.

You know you have a child with severe reflux when...

You nod and smile while friends, relatives and strangers tell
you, "She looks so healthy" and "She doesn't look sick."

Your baby is inconsolable for hours at a time, vomits 30+
times a day and does not sleep more than an hour and the
pediatrician says, "All babies" cry, vomit and wake up at
night.

Your husband, friends, neighbors and grandparents refuse to
be left alone with your high-need baby and those who do
come to help never return after one day.

You have to buy a new car seat every few months because the
old one reeks of vomit and special formula.

You struggle to stay awake while driving home from the food
store at 2 o'clock in the afternoon, sure that a policeman will
pull you over for weaving and revoke your license on the
spot.

You have not had a full night of sleep in _____ (fill in the
blank) years and you know the sleep deprivation studies are
correct.

Your baby vomits so much she has ruined a chair and the new
carpeting and you both run out of clean clothes by 10am
each day.

You log on to the internet at your first opportunity (say,
11:30pm), seeking support/info. Sometimes you hold the
baby over your shoulder with one hand and hunt and peck
with the other hand.

You finally get out, enjoying a leisurely lunch with the other
reflux moms. Half way through the meal, you realize that the
other patrons in the restaurant are listening in horror to your
conversation containing graphic descriptions of body fluids-

color, quantity, frequency, amount of blood, which end, etc
You think this is funny.

After caring for your inconsolable baby 24/7, you know why
babies are shaken or worse by their parents.

Instead of joining the moms and tots playgroup or the PTA,
you joined PAGER, Mothers of Asthmatics and the Food and
Allergy Network.

You have taken multi-tasking to a new and dangerous level.
You always have a contingency plan.

You have watched Toy Story 68 times, quote Disney movies at
cocktail parties and hum the theme song while during
laundry. All because you and your child have watched far
too many videos during frequent, prolonged illnesses.

Instead of reading, "What to Expect in the First Year", your
parent bookshelf contains: Physician Desk Reference, a good
medical dictionary and the Merck Manual (physicians
edition, not the home edition).

You keep meticulous records. You are sure your child's food
intake record contains clues for an effective weight loss
plan. You plan to publish it, make a lot of money and appear
on Oprah.

The baby book is full of cute mementoes: hospital bracelets, a
picture with Santa on Christmas morning in the children's
ward, and discharge orders from surgery.

Your pediatric gastroenterologist carries your child's records
with him at all times. He tells you his vacation/leave plans
before the front office staff knows.

Your child's medical records at the pediatrician's office are so
large, it has to be divided into Part I and Part II by the time
your child is 7 years old.

You've fired some doctors, had heated debates with others
and stood your ground when the doctor dismissed your
concerns or tried to discharge you too early. You know the
saying is true, when you have a sick kid, "Don't mess with
the mama lion."

You are positively ecstatic when both the specialists can see
your child on the same day at the children's hospital an hour
away. Imagine what you will do with all of that free time!

To visit grandma, Disneyworld or go camping for the weekend, you pack a large tote bag full of medicine, syringes, tubing, stethoscope, and starter supply of antibiotics, AC adapter for the durable medical equipment, a case of special formula, a feeding pump and a nebulizer. You worry that you have left something vital behind.

The FAA issues a travel alert warning of delays when your family plans to travel by air due to the excess baggage and security screening involved.

You don't have to "panic buy" before a snowstorm or hurricane. You learned a long time ago to be prepared: for sudden illness, a trip to the hospital and being homebound for days or weeks at a time. What's a little hurricane?!

The drugstore pharmacist at the mega-food store knows you by name despite the fact that they fill thousands of prescriptions per month. On average, for every $100 you spend on groceries, you spent $50.00 on medication and formula.

You pack an overnight bag before a sick visit to the pediatrician. Often, you need it and wish you had packed more chocolate bars.

Your little gerdling has 50+ doctor/clinic appointments and 75+ prescription refills per year.

An overnight stay at the hospital feels like a mini vacation after managing your child's illness at home. Reality sets in when you are discharged and resume your 24 hour duties as pediatrician, nurse, gastroenterologist, dietician, pharmacist, respiratory therapist, social worker, case manager, housekeeper, laundry aide, video changer on top of your other household/family duties. You envy the nurses who get to go home after a 12 hour shift.

You know you will survive this because of your friends, family and organizations such as PAGER Association are there to support and guide you.

You and your child have developed a special bond. You wonder if you would cherish your child as much if her chronic condition hadn't forced you to spend so much time together.

You wonder if you would have learned to live in the present and appreciate the little things if your child didn't have a chronic illness.

You didn't think your life would be like this. You have no regrets and wouldn't change one little thing.

Jan Gambino

▶ INDEX

achalasia. *See* Lower
  Esophageal Sphincter (LES)
advice
  from doctors, 102, 124, 128,
    182
  from experts, 47, 90, 105-06
  from family and friends,
    135, 151, 154-56, 183
  trusting your instincts with,
    80, 87, 138, 141, 146-47
advocacy, 19, 25, 54, 92, 95,
  106-07, 109-10
  problems with medication,
    121
  See also documentation;
    advice, trusting your
    instincts with
air intake. *See* feeding
alcohol and reflux, 176
alkaline reflux, 66
American Academy of
  Pediatrics. *See* Back to Sleep
  Campaign
anger and frustration, 1, 102-
  104, 146, 164, 190
  and abuse, 136-38
  and relationships, 135, 139,
    149, 152, 155, 156
  a child's, 55, 120, 172, 174
  See also exhaustion

apnea, 61, 93, 106, 110, 172,
  230
  See also breathing;
    complications, respiratory
Apparent Life Threatening
  Event (ALTE), 61, 93, 230
arching back. *See* pain
asthma, 60-61, 106, 217, 226,
  230, 234
  See also breathing;
    complications, respiratory
autism, 70-71
Back to Sleep Campaign, 38,
  40
backwash, 9, 53, 73, 169, 172,
  178, 206, 224
  See also vomiting
bad breath. *See* complications,
  dental
Barrett's Esophagus, 63, 172,
  230
behavior, as a symptom, 17,
  56, 80, 93, 109
behavior issues, child's, 73,
  106, 119, 120, 152, 171-182
bloating. *See* gastric
  discomfort
breastfeeding, 46-50, 55, 79
  effects of, 41, 43, 83, 135
  specialist, 50